GARDEN TOOLS

GARDEN TOOLS

VAL BRADLEY & JOHN NEGUS

LAUREL
GLEN

San Diego, California

I wish to dedicate this book to my dear wife, Phyll, who
supported and encouraged me throughout our life together.
John Negus

Laurel Glen Publishing
An imprint of the Advantage Publishers Group
5880 Oberlin Drive, San Diego, CA 92121–4794
www.advantagebooksonline.com

Illustrations and Compilation Copyright © Carroll & Brown
Limited, 2001
Text Copyright © Val Bradley and John Negus, 2001

Created and produced by:
Carroll & Brown Limited
20 Lonsdale Road, Queen's Park, London NW6 6RD, UK

Editor Helen Griffin
Art Editor Vimit Punater
Photography David Murray and Jules Selmes

All notations of errors or omissions should be addressed to Laurel
Glen Publishing, editorial department, at the above address. All other
correspondence (author inquiries, permissions and rights) concerning
the content of this book should be addressed to Carroll & Brown
Publishers Limited, 20 Lonsdale Road, Queen's Park, London NW6
6RD, England.

ISBN 1-57145-584-1
Library of Congress Cataloging-in-Publication Data available
upon request.

Printed in Spain.
1 2 3 4 5   01 02 03 04 05

Contents

Introduction

Ask anyone who has been gardening for a while about their favorite tool, and they will always have one. It might be a brand-new implement that makes working easier, but it's just as likely to be one passed down from another avid gardener in the family. Many a gardener has a treasured family spade, for instance, which has been repaired so many times over the years—with a new handle here and a new head there—that it is actually a completely different tool. Yet it will still feel like the same much-loved spade to its owner.

To the uninitiated, the selection of tools available today can be vast and bewildering. Even an apparently simple item, such as a hand trowel, comes in a wide variety of styles and brands. What is the optimum shape and size? Is there any advantage in choosing one kind of blade over another? What kind of handle should it have?

Selecting the best tool for each job means that you can execute the task with minimum effort and maximum pleasure. This book details how to use each tool and the uses to which each tool is best suited (so you don't have to struggle with the wrong one). The first few chapters look at implements for all the important tasks in the garden: digging (Chapter 1); cultivating and weeding (Chapter 2); watering, reading the weather, and greenhouse equipment (Chapter 3); cutting and trimming the lawn and your plants (Chapter 4); planting and sowing (Chapter 5); and tidying the garden (clearing, hauling, and composting: Chapter 6). Safety is the subject of Chapter 7, which covers such issues as wearing protective gear, working with electricity and chemicals, and ensuring the garden is safe when children or pets are around. And Chapters 8 and 9 offer advice on tools that make your life easier, and maintenance and storage, respectively. Interspersed throughout are features on specialized tools for hobbyists (such as bonsai, water gardens, and roses).

Whether you are building a collection from scratch, or simply looking to add to or get the most from your existing tool kit, we hope that this book will help to ensure that gardening is always a source of pleasure and never a chore.

1

Digging In

Improving the soil

Ever since our ancestors began to grow plants for food, they recognized the need to cultivate the soil. The simple fact is that plants grow better in properly prepared ground. The earliest cultivation tools included sticks and large animal bones. But successive generations have refined the tools to the spades, shovels, forks, and mattocks that we use today.

The best way of improving most soils is to take a spade to them and start digging. The purpose of turning the dirt, whether it is to one spade's depth (a process known as "single digging") or two ("double digging"), is to put air into it, and whether you enjoy the task or dread it, turning soil is a necessary part of the gardening year.

WHY DO YOU NEED TO DIG?

Air is critical to plant roots, and without it the plants would die. A lack of air in the soil is often caused by compaction, which occurs naturally, particularly in areas of high rainfall or where land is often trodden.

Digging and turning the soil, especially in the fall, enables the freezing action of winter frosts to break down larger clumps and create new air pockets between the particles making the soil easier for the roots to penetrate. It plays an important part in the organic cycle within the soil, allowing the burying of crop and plant debris, weeds, and organic wastes, such as manure or garden compost.

It also aids beneficial soil organisms, such as worms and bacteria, which must have air in order to live. These creatures break down organic waste and open up the soil further to incorporate more air and allow rainwater to drain away more freely.

Drainage is an important consideration if you live in an area where the level of rainfall is high, or on a heavy, clay soil that is prone to waterlogging. Regular digging is essential to the structure of these soils, and should be done on an annual basis wherever possible—especially in highly productive areas such as the vegetable patch. In an established shrub border, where the plants are to remain in place for a number of years, it is more important to prepare the ground thoroughly before planting begins.

Spades and shovels

When sharp and well maintained, these tools
can perform myriad tasks in your garden—
from, of course, turning and scooping up soil
to leveling your borders or scraping out
debris between paving stones.

Creating good soil

Lift and aerate the soil with the help of a
spade or fork. You can incorporate good-
quality compost at the same time to further
improve the quality of the soil.

SPADES

The average spade is an upright implement with a flat, rectangular blade that you can push straight down into the soil with your foot. Once the blade is in the soil, lever the handle back to lift a section of soil free from the main area to be turned over.

In days gone by, each job in the garden had its own implement (as well as a person to do it!). There were separate spades for turning the soil, digging ditches, planting trees, cutting peat or turf, tidying the edges of borders, and shoveling potatoes into sacks. Thankfully, advances in tool design and manufacture mean that one spade is sufficient for most modern gardeners. This is just as well, because few of us today have the space to store all those separate tools.

The basic design for the digging spade has become fairly standard throughout the world, although finer points of the design have been adapted in some areas to accommodate different local soil conditions and the particular crops grown.

The standard (sometimes called "English garden") spade will suit most purposes. Substantial, heavy-weight, and yet well balanced, this is probably the model to choose if you want only one spade. If you find this type too unwieldy or too large for the size of your flower beds, however, consider a border spade, which is simply a scaled-down version of the English Garden spade. For those with infinite space in the tool shed, a rootball spade is a worthwhile investment.

A good handle, which can come in a T-, D-, or YD-shape, should be comfortable to hold and, the shaft of the spade you choose should allow your hand to fit loosely. Wood is the most common material for the shaft, but metal and fiberglass are stronger and may be more suitable if you do a lot of heavy digging work.

A solid, forged head is more durable than those stamped out from a metal sheet and is best when reinforced in areas of high strain.

With its extra-long, narrow head, it makes quick work of digging deep holes for plants or garden structures. Various long-handled spades are also available for jobs requiring extra leverage, or for particularly long-legged gardeners.

Digging spades are versatile tools, and make an important contribution to many of the routine tasks in the garden, although you should not use them on really stony soil, as the extra leverage needed may strain the handle and damage it.

Extending the gardener's arm

Almost any digging tool you can think of— be it spade, shovel, hoe, or fork—is loosely modeled on the capability of your own two hands. They are simply designed to improve upon them!

> **"I wish with all my heart that I were a man, for of course the first thing I should do would be to buy a spade and go and garden."**
>
> COUNTESS VON ARNIM, NOVELIST (1866–1941)

PLANTING AND DIGGING UP

Spades are the first choice for digging planting holes when the most important consideration is to create a hole large enough to accommodate the rootball of the new plant. You simply push the blade of the spade into the ground with the sole of your foot, lever the handle back toward you to loosen the soil, then bend your knees as you lift the soil clear of the hole. Keep the soil nearby in a heap and mix it with compost or a planting mixture before replacing it around the roots of the new plant. Disperse any surplus soil around your garden.

Spades are also useful for digging up plants, especially where you want to keep the rootball intact. Drive the spade vertically down into the soil in a circle around the plant you are lifting, without removing any soil. Gradually, begin to lever the plant upward, so that you can work the spade underneath the roots. Sever any thick anchoring roots cleanly until you can lift the plant out of the ground.

SINGLE DIGGING

The task of preparing the ground in the fall for planting the following spring will always be easier if you use a clean, sharp spade to turn over the soil. The simplest method is single digging, which involves turning the topsoil to the depth of one spade blade: See below. This action places the previous surface soil (and any weed seeds on it) several inches below the new surface. Most weeds will not have the light they

WHAT CAN YOU DO WITH A SPADE?

- Create planting holes for new plant arrivals.
- Dig around a plant prior to transferring it or binding its rootball.
- Single dig.
- Double dig.
- Move quantities of soil or compost around the work area.
- Skim off turf or weeds from an area's surface.

Single digging

1 **LOOSEN COMPACTED SOIL** Push the spade's blade down into the soil with your foot and lever the handle toward you to break up the clumps of soil.

2 **LIFTING THE SOIL** Bend your knees and, keeping your back straight, lift the soil clear. Work on small amounts of soil at a time to avoid straining your back.

3 **TURNING OVER** As you replace it on the ground, invert it by twisting the spade handle over toward you. Work backward so you don't stand on the soil you have just turned. This is demanding work, particularly in areas of heavy soil, so take regular breaks.

Coming up roses

Having planted your rose bushes and climbers in a sunny, fertile, well-drained spot, it's easy enough to achieve a dazzling display. Pleasingly, few tools are needed to keep them shapely and performing well. These are a few of your allies.

Rose pruning, the subject of many a solemn masterclass and well-thumbed pages in pruning manuals, is nowadays greatly demystified after trials found that a quick "shave" with a hedge trimmer was actually more effective than any precise, long-considered cuts to individual rose stems. However, for a neat and tidy trim, pruning shears will always be the best tool to use—and they leave none of the messy-looking jagged edges that hedge trimmers do.

For pruning your roses, use anvil shears or side-anvil pruners, which have a honed cutting edge that slices against a thick blade. If you have large beds and borders of roses, consider investing in a pair of side-anvil shears with a rotating handle to reduce the strain on your

Hose-end feeder
Mix liquid foliar feed in a diluter attachment on the end of a hose. Spray the liquid feed directly onto the rose (right) throughout the flowering season to stimulate further flushes of bloom.

In training

Weeping roses are given form and structure by using an "umbrella" or "basket" frame. Secure your rose to a central column and, using soft string, tie the shoots to the frame. Lightly prune a weeping standard with a sharp pair of pruning shears.

wrist as well as the risk of blisters. Periodically, tough, old shoots need clipping to spur new growth from the base. Use strong long-handled shears rather than pruning shears. Choose a pair with lightweight aluminum handles and a cantilever cutting action to increase leverage.

The best saw to prune the limbs off rose shrubs is the safe, fold-up version with a high-carbon and nonclogging steel blade and a set of precision-ground, razor-sharp teeth. Buy one with a safety catch to secure the blade.

Rose training

Reminiscent of a skeletal, wire, hanging basket, with or without a central pole, a rose trainer is positioned over the head of a standard weeping rose to provide ornamental support. New shoots tied to it are trained to form an umbrella of flowering branches.

Classical obelisks are pillars entwined with the spiraling shoots of climbing roses in various heights and diameters. The best modern types use plastic-coated 1-inch steel tubing linked with metal rings, topped with a molded finial.

Twine is essential for tying in young stems—they should be trained as horizontally as possible to encourage a wealth of blossom. It's best to use organic, jute twine, which can then be composted when you replace it.

Whenever you work with roses, you must wear heavy-duty, thornproof gloves to guard against cutting your fingers. You should also wear safety goggles, as shoots can fly from your grasp and into your face. Choose a pair with adjustable arms and lenses.

Backpack sprayer

Most roses need spraying with fungicide and insecticide. The most efficient way to do this is with a pump-up, backpack sprayer. Contoured to fit your back, it comes with a heavy-duty pump handle to reduce effort. Accessories include an extension lance and fan spray nozzle.

Propagation

If you're interested in increasing a hybrid tea rose variety that is budded onto a stock plant, you'll need a sharp, flat-bladed budding knife with a thumb grip. It should have a flat-ended handle for prying up the T-shaped cut you make in the bark to insert the bud.

Building up and cutting down

Wrap your roses in horticultural crop-protection fleece for the winter (above), and be sure to cover any young shoots if there are frosts forecast. Use shears (above left) or loppers to tackle those with thick stems.

need to germinate, but even if some do start to grow, they seldom have the energy to push through the extra depth of soil and reach the surface. An important tip is to work backward rather than forward: turning the soil introduces air into it, but by standing on it too quickly you can squash the air straight back out, leaving it compacted.

DOUBLE DIGGING

Also known as deep digging, this process of aerating and amending the soil is especially useful on heavy clay soils that form sticky lumps and resist all efforts to break them into a fine tilth with crumbly texture. It is best carried out in the fall so that winter frosts can break down larger clods for you.

As the name suggests, this technique involves digging down to the depth of two spade blades instead of just one. To double dig, you need to excavate a spade-deep trench, putting the soil to one side, and then dig down another spade's depth to work the soil at the bottom of the trench. Next, you dig a second trench, adjacent to the first one, turning the topsoil you excavate from this into the previous trench. Once you have loosened the subsoil at the bottom of this second trench, you can use the soil from the first one to fill the last one (for step-by-step instructions, see below).

The soil at the bottom of the trench is known as subsoil; this is a much less fertile medium, but it holds the most moisture. For good plant growth, roots must penetrate this subsoil to keep supplied with water, even in summer.

Keep topsoil and subsoil separate at all times as you are working. Mixing them together will not improve the fertility of the subsoil—as was believed for a time—instead it will dilute that of the topsoil.

OTHER USES

The spade is a versatile tool, and you don't just have to use it for digging; it is also helpful for moving quantities of soil or compost around the garden, or for skimming the turf or weeds off the surface of an area before you construct the base of a new building or dig out a pond. Do this by holding the spade so that it is almost parallel to the ground and sliding it under the top inch of the soil with quick, sharp pushes. You can reuse any turf you take off in this manner elsewhere in the garden.

The weight of the spade makes it a handy tool for breaking up clods, tapping down soil, paving stones, and other garden material—be careful not to damage it though. The straight-cutting blade can be used to create neat-edged borders, to cut through weeds, and to pry up rocks and stones.

Double digging

1 **MARKING OUT** Start by marking out the area to be dug, as you will be working up one side and back down the other.

2 **DIG A TRENCH** Follow the instructions for single digging (page 13), but instead of replacing the topsoil, put it into a wheelbarrow and keep it to one side.

3 **IMPROVE ROOT PENETRATION** Use a fork to loosen the subsoil at the bottom of the trench, pushing it down to the full depth of its tines. Lift the soil, then let it fall back, breaking it up by turning the fork over and using the prongs on any larger clods. This cultivates the soil to two blades' depth. Place a generous layer of well-rotted manure or garden compost onto the bottom of the trench.

4 **WORK ON THE SECOND TRENCH** Using the spade, dig the next trench, but this time throw the topsoil into the first trench, and mix it thoroughly with the compost or manure. Work around the plot until you reach the last trench, finishing off by using the topsoil taken from the first trench.

SHOVELS

This is a different implement depending upon which side of the Atlantic Ocean you garden. In the U.K., a standard shovel is a wide, almost square-bladed implement used for moving larger quantities of material around than a spade will hold. You would seldom use it for "proper" gardening activities and are more likely to find it useful when mixing concrete or moving organic matter. The Cornish spade is a long-handled shovel with a blade tapering to a point.

The American shovel closely resembles a traditional Cornish spade (from which it probably evolved with the early settlers), with a long, straight handle and a concave, pointed blade that can enter the soil with impressive force.

The shovel is most useful as a scooping tool, for which it is conveniently dish-shaped. Its concave blade holds soil more efficiently than the flatter spade, which is why it is the tool of choice for many gardeners. The pointed blade will cut through compacted soil more easily than the spade, but is probably less useful for pure digging because it does not produce a straight edge. It is a multifunctional tool, however, and can do anything a rectangular spade can do in terms of lifting, moving, planting, transplanting, and mixing materials.

The shovel's long handle means that gardeners of any height can use it—unlike the spade handle, which is of a set length. It also allows you to shift your grip according to the weight you are lifting, or the soil you are trying to cultivate.

To use a shovel, rest your foot on the tread of the blade, hold the shaft up vertically, and use your body weight to push the blade down into the soil. Then

The great American shovel
The long handle allows you to adjust your grip as appropriate, while the wide, bowl-shaped dish enables you to carry material without spilling it.

stand up straight, and use the long handle as a lever, pulling it toward you to loosen the soil. Bend at the knees to pick up a small scoop, and then swivel at the hips to dispose of the material. Remember always to bend your legs rather than your back to avoid injury.

Use your shovel to move piles of soil, compost, plant matter such as grass clippings, sand or any other material. For comfort and efficiency, keep shovelfuls small and light, working regularly and, if possible, rapidly, to reduce the pile.

The best shovels have heads made from a single piece of forged steel that have been thickened at the points of greatest stress where the shovel might bend. If you have a choice of tread, opt for a forward-rolled tread, which will protect the soles of your boots from shock or stress during repeated digging.

WHAT CAN YOU DO WITH A SHOVEL?
- Loosen soil surface before planting or adding dry fertilizer.
- Cultivate the soil.
- Lift and throw substantial piles of organic matter.
- Transplant and plant perennials and shrubs in the garden.
- Mix concrete.
- Slice finger-sized underground roots during digging.

FORKS

The basic design of the fork is fairly universal, with a long, straight handle and four metal prongs or tines. The prongs vary according to the intended use of the fork: A digging fork has square-profile tines for the soil to cling to; the circular prongs of the pitchfork help the soil slide off; and the flat tines in others such as the potato or beet fork avoid damage to the crop.

WHAT CAN YOU DO WITH A FORK?

- Loosen soil surface before planting or adding dry fertilizer.
- Cultivate in confined spaces between fragile plants in the border.
- Spike a lawn to improve drainage (before brushing in sand).
- Penetrate the bottom of a trench during double digging.
- Lift and transport cartfuls of manure and other organic matter.
- Lift root vegetables, including potatoes and carrots.

Picking your pitchfork

The shape and size of prongs can make a big difference to your tasks: arched tines scoop up material effectively; short, blunt prongs help prevent damage to tender bulbs; and flat edges dig well, as the soil clings easily.

Prongs are angled according to the fork's purpose—straight tines are best for digging and arched ones for scooping.

The so-called garden fork, with four prongs, is the heaviest-duty model, and the tool of choice for gardeners who do a lot of double digging. Spading, digging, and border forks are similar to garden forks but smaller, lighter, and a little less resilient. These make good all-purpose tools. Where space is restricted, a border fork is smaller and will fit between the plants more easily.

Other forks for lifting manure and bedding have between five and ten tines, and are used primarily for animal bedding and waste. However, they are quite useful in the garden for moving bulk quantities of material around, such as mulch, compost, or leaves, or for lifting small root crops like new potatoes, which would fall through the gaps between the tines of a standard digging fork. Pitchforks tend to have just two or three long prongs and a long handle, perfect for lifting hay and light-weight mulches.

Use a potato fork to pry out root vegetables, such as beets, carrots, and potatoes from the soil. The five or six prongs are blunt, so they won't damage the crop.

Like the spade, the fork serves several purposes. Use a garden fork for loosening the soil's surface—where deep digging is not possible between established plants in the border—and especially when adding dry fertilizer to the upper layer of soil around plants. Always work backward so that you do not stand on, and thereby recompress, soil that has been dug over.

SPIKING A LAWN

You can instantly improve a poorly draining lawn area by "spiking" it with a fork—simply drive the prongs down into the grass to their full depth with your foot. You can leave the resulting holes open, or for a more permanent solution, fill them with sand. Brush the sand over the lawn's surface making sure it goes down into the holes.

The fork is also ideal for rough leveling a cultivated area after you have dug it and before you start to lay turf, plant out, or sow seed. However, final leveling is best done with a rake.

RELIEVING COMPACTION

Where the fork really comes into its own is for deep cultivation of the soil in "double digging" (see page 16). The garden fork has a great ability to penetrate compacted layers of soil because each slender tine can exert tremendous pressure through its pointed tip. This allows you to break through the initial compaction, lift the soil, and then break it into smaller clods. By turning the fork over and hitting the lumps of soil with the points of the tines, you can reduce the lumps to a manageable size.

Aerating your lawn

Use your body weight on a garden fork to make holes in your lawn, then move the handle around slightly to enlarge them. Brush sand into the holes for good drainage.

MATTOCKS AND PICKS

Spades and forks are good for most digging purposes, but some jobs require an altogether tougher tool. This is where the mattock or pick comes in.

Though not the most-used tools in the garden shed, mattocks and picks will be invaluable at certain times in a larger garden. These are heavy-duty implements designed for cutting through solid soil or thick roots with ease, although in some parts of the world where the soil is thin and stony, a broad-bladed, hoe-like mattock is used in place of a spade for basic cultivation.

The difference between these two implements lies in their shape. The pick has a strong wooden handle and a metal head with two pointed ends, one sharp, the other squared. It is an ideal implement for digging a trench, especially through compacted, stony ground. Raise it and swing it down in a circular motion, with one hand remaining at the base of the handle while the other slides up and down to control the swing.

In contrast, the head of the mattock has one chisel-pointed end while the other is flattened into a cutting blade. It is a combination of useful cultivator for stony areas and sturdy tool for lifting or cutting through stubborn roots or brambles.

The standard mattock can perform a variety of cultivating tasks. It can dig in and break up soil, cut through obstructive roots, and push or pull rocks and stones out of the way. More specialty mattocks are also available from some manufacturers. Short-handled bedding mattocks have a pointed, trowel-shaped head to make a plant-size hole in the soil; and certain models have a fork-like head with narrow tines, which are useful for breaking up clumps of soil without gathering up soil.

Both tools require a reasonable amount of strength to use, and good technique is essential if you are to avoid injury. Work with a steady rhythm to avoid jerking and straining your back, and be sure to keep a tight hold of the handle.

Picks gather a great deal of force as you swing them in a circular motion, so make sure the head is firmly mounted on the shaft before each use for safety.

CHOOSING THE RIGHT TOOLS

To do any physical job properly—with a minimum of impact to your body—it is essential to have a tool that suits both you and the work you are planning to undertake. A tall person cannot work efficiently when employing a short-handled spade, and, equally, a small-framed person will find the job much harder if using a large, heavy spade.

Before buying a digging tool, such as a spade or fork, there are a number of things to find out and consider. The first thing to be done, if at all possible, is to practice with the tools themselves to gauge their weight and balance.

Look for a combination of strength and lightness. Try borrowing tools from gardening friends who have experience in using them, or visit a range of tool centers and try as many different makes as possible for weight and balance. Hold them, bend over with them, lift them—in fact, do all the things you will do once you buy them. Don't worry about looking foolish in the store—the right tool is an investment and needs appropriate research, because the wrong tool could cause you hours of aches and pains.

In each case, the straight handle connects to the heavy head by passing through an "eye" in the center of the head itself. This means that if the handle is damaged, you can easily replace it. You should check the shaft regularly, particularly if it is made of wood, to ensure it is smooth and free of splinters. Dry it carefully before putting it into storage to prevent the wood from rotting or shrinking. If the handle shows any sign at all of shrinking within the eye, replace it, because the last thing you'll need is the head flying off while the tool is in use.

Strong joints

Digging implements are subject to considerable pressure, so it is important that the blade or head is firmly attached to the handle. The two strongest joints are the socket (right) and the saddle (far right).

JOINTS

Look at the joint between the head (the tines of a fork or the blade of a spade) and the handle. Check that it is firm and secure, or the two may part company as you are working.

There are two main methods of attaching the head to the shaft: the socket joint and the saddle joint. Both types of attachment are strong and should withstand years of heavy use.

With a socket joint, the handle fits into a circular hole at the top of the head and is secured in place with rivets driven through the shaft. A socket fitting may be long or short; the longer the socket, the less handle there will be, and the stronger the implement. Lipped sockets have a short strap at the front and back to increase their strength.

In the case of the saddle joint, two straps come up from the head and lie against the front and back of the handle, secured with two or more rivets.

You may come across tools where the head is a cut-out piece of metal that has been folded into shape around the handle, leaving a hollow indentation at the back. This design is unlikely to be expensive—but will probably not last very long. It may be ideal for building sand castles on the beach, but it's best to avoid it for the garden.

CHOOSE HANDLES WITH CARE

Examine the shaft of the implement to check that all of the surfaces are smooth, as this will help to avoid injury to your hands. Pay particular attention to the handle or grip, as a smooth, well-made handle will greatly reduce the risk of painful blisters as you work. Handles with a Y- or T-shaped grip have been around since the days of the Roman Empire. Most heavy-duty garden tools today have D-, YD- (wishbone-shaped), or T-shaped handles, and the one you choose will be based on comfort and personal preference (see picture, above). Try the grip for size before you buy the implement, because a narrow one may be difficult to use if you prefer to work with gardening gloves, and a chunky one may be too large if you have small hands. Ergonomic grips to make working easier are angled forward slightly, away from the body.

The grip itself may be made of weather-proofed wood (usually ash), tubular metal, or polypropylene (which may have an integral molded grip). Modern polypropylene grips are molded in one continuous hollow piece by gas injection. They are smooth, strong, and created at an ideal digging angle. They can even be UV- and fade-resistant, and are recyclable.

WHAT SIZE OF TOOL?

Spades and forks come in three basic sizes: small, medium, and large. The smallest is sometimes called border size, and the largest is digging size. Which size you choose will depend on you and your garden. If your garden is large and needs a lot of maintenance, then your tools will have to be big and strong enough to cope. If, on the other hand, your garden is small and confined, then the tools will have to be correspondingly smaller, and a border size may be more suitable.

Choose a size and weight that you can work with comfortably for as long as it takes to finish the job. Some manufacturers have taken into account the

THE MAKING OF SPADES

Metal garden tools, which date back to Roman times, would once have been the province of the local craftsman-cum-blacksmith. He would have been able to melt down and reuse broken tools to make new ones.

Mass production of garden tools began in the nineteenth century in response to the huge interest in gardening as a leisure pursuit. The big advances in manufacture since then have been in the materials used to produce the tools, reducing the weight of each tool dramatically. The design has changed just slightly, although it is now possible to buy tools with a built-in grip for the foot to press down on, to make digging easier.

Many tools today are made of carbon steel, a mixture of carbon and mild steel that is heat-treated and tempered for strength. Mild steel alone would rust overnight without protection.

Hand-forging spades

Made using techniques passed down by generations of blacksmiths, handmade spades and hoes are in great demand for their quality and durability.

1 **THE BASIC SHAPE** First, stainless steel spade heads are clipped into shape, ready to be put in the fire.

2 **HEATING THE METAL** The heads are then fired until red-hot and suitably malleable to be beaten and molded.

3 **THE HARDENING PROCESS** To withstand heavy use, the blade has to be hardened by means of compression, followed by heat and rapid cooling. The tool is then dipped in acid leaving it shiny and new.

gradual increase in average height of the population, and offer a range of tools suited to taller gardeners. Their longer length encourages a more upright working stance and reduces the risk of backache. Spades and shovels are available with a straight shaft up to 6 feet long, and, as well as suiting taller people, these are useful for providing good leverage during deeper digging.

THE TOOL HEAD

Digging tools are generally made from steel, which comes in various types and grades (see right). Top-of-the-range tools are generally made from stainless steel, but high-carbon models are also good quality and won't set you back as much.

Tempered or forged implements are preferable over stamped ones (which are machine cut and bent to the required shape) as they are better designed to withstand hard use.

When buying tools, look to see if the head is coated. Many carbon-steel heads are given a special epoxy paint coating to lengthen their lifetime. As well as reducing the chance of soil sticking to the head, this coating will make the tool lighter and easier to use. It should also guard against rust, scratching, and the effects of humidity and alkalis in the soil.

COUNTING THE COST

The final consideration is one of cost, and in this instance, you really do get what you pay for. If you have a tiny garden, which is largely made up of hard surfaces and with just a small area of planting to be looked after, then it is unlikely to be worth your while spending a fortune on stainless-steel tools. If your garden is large, or you intend to produce and maintain a viable vegetable patch, then cheaper tools are likely to last for perhaps three seasons before they bend or

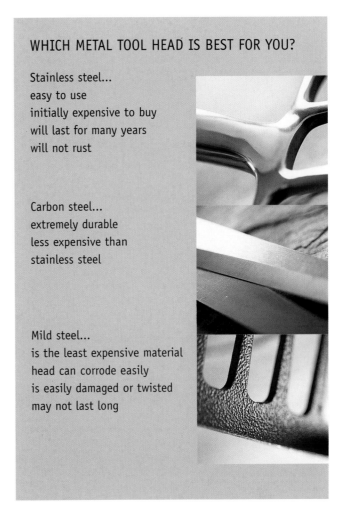

WHICH METAL TOOL HEAD IS BEST FOR YOU?

Stainless steel...
easy to use
initially expensive to buy
will last for many years
will not rust

Carbon steel...
extremely durable
less expensive than
stainless steel

Mild steel...
is the least expensive material
head can corrode easily
is easily damaged or twisted
may not last long

break. It all depends on how much you use the tools, and for what. Used correctly, stainless steel tools (the most expensive option) should last you a lifetime and will be a good investment. They also make a wonderful present for the new gardener who is just starting out. For advice on how to look after your tools, whatever their shape or material, see Chapter 9 (pages 146–151).

>tools of the future

The days of wooden tools may be numbered. Manufacturers are looking at the possibility of using plastics to form the whole implement, not just the handle. From their point of view, the problem is that these tools would have a much longer life and would be almost indestructible. Great news for the consumer though!

2

Cultivating the Soil

Tools for weeding

One square yard of soil can hold an average of 50,000 viable seeds a year, and as soon as you break the surface of the soil, seeds in the upper layers receive the daylight they need to germinate. Add to these the weeds that creep under the fence from your neighbor's garden and those the birds leave behind as they fly over, and you will have a good crop of weeds in your garden!

CULTIVATING GOOD HABITS

Once you start to cultivate your soil, you must continue, but a little-and-often approach means that it need not become a battle. It is up to you to ensure that weed seedlings do not compete for the limited light, moisture, and nutrients available for the plants that you do want to grow. The best way to make sure of this is to cultivate the soil around your plants using hoes, rakes, cultivators, trowels, and hand forks.

Well-made joints

Hoes, rakes, and cultivators with wooden (usually ash) handles all tend to have a tang-and-ferrule fitting for extra strength, with the joint just above the head. Where the shaft is aluminum or polypropylene, the joint is a socket fitting. Whichever you choose, make

---

UNDERSTANDING THE ORGANIC CYCLE

The plants that start to grow send their questing roots down into the first covering, sucking up moisture and breaking down the bedrock further. When they die, they decay into organic matter that feeds both the new plants and the organisms in the soil. When the organisms die, they, in turn, form nutrients that the plants can use. The leaves that fall from the plants form a natural mulch over the soil and are gradually taken down and incorporated into the soil by the organisms that dwell there. This cycle is repeated every year, building up the soil unless there is some outside interference to affect the process.

Handling a hoe

The perennially popular Dutch hoe is used with a push-pull action. It cuts weeds down to size before they start to compete for nutrients and moisture with plants you want to grow. Ensure your hoe is light enough to be wielded by your arms rather than your back, which should be kept straight.

and the ferrule is a metal ring that is designed to be fitted down over the joint to hold it closed and prevent the wood from parting.

HOES

The humble hoe is a versatile implement, ideal for light, regular, ground cultivation. Use it to control weeds and loosen the soil around the base of plants. Most have a long, straight handle with a metal head, but there are many designs from around the world that were developed to take account of local conditions. The three most common designs are the Dutch hoe, the draw (or swan-neck) hoe, and the triangular-headed hoe.

Which one you use will be a matter of personal preference as much as a selection based on technical use. It may even be a regional variation, with local history and soil conditions dictating which hoes are available for purchase. The Dutch hoe is a good starting point for general gardening, as it can cope with most soils, from a light sandy loam to a fairly heavy clay, and can be turned slightly so that the corner of the blade will make an adequate drill if you want to sow seed. If you are growing vegetables or have lumpy soil, you may wish to add a draw hoe to your collection, as it is useful for breaking clods, earthing up, and will produce a finer drill for sowing small seeds.

WHEELED HOE

This device is for the gardener who wishes to cultivate a large area, as it is not easy to maneuver between

sure that the joint is tight and well-made. A poor fitting will not last long, and may part company just when you least wish it. When considering a hoe, rake, or cultivator, ensure that the tool is light enough for your arms to wield it (rather than your back) and that the handle is a comfortable length. Tools are generally lightweight and the heads are made of stainless steel or carbon steel coated with a protective epoxy paint, which makes the tool easier to handle by reducing soil adhesion.

What to look for in a hand tool

The shaft may be treated wood (usually ash), aluminum, or polypropylene—and the grip, if there is one, is usually polypropylene. The head may be attached to the shaft with a socket fitting (where the head has a circular hole into which the shaft is pushed and held in place with rivets), or, where the shaft is wood, a tang-and-ferrule. The tang is a sharp point on the top of the head that fits into the base of the shaft,

"Whatever hour the sun may say, it's always time for weeding;
The dandelion which blooms today, tomorrow will be seeding."
A.A. MILNE, WRITER AND POET (1882–1956)

Bonsai tools

Bonsai, or the ancient Eastern art of dwarfing trees, is not a hobby to hurry. It can take a lifetime of commitment to truly understand this complex and beautiful art form. But knowing the right tools to use can give you a head start.

The addictive art form of bonsai was pioneered in the Far East, around 1000 years ago, and literally means "a tree" (*sai*) "growing in glazed terra-cotta tray or pot" (*bon*). The challenge is to replicate in miniature the trunk, shoots, leaves, and flowers of a tree, bush, or climber that, in struggling to survive in the cleft of a rock, has become gnarled, contorted, and curiously beautiful.

Good contenders are trees such as maple, Japanese white pine, Chinese elm, Chinese juniper, crab apple, azalea, beech, and hornbeam. They will, given dedication, grow to awesome veterans: a centenarian bonsai pine is not uncommon.

The key to keeping a tree small, healthy, and mimicking its ancient, craggy wildwood cousin, is the care you give it. Prune it regularly and train its shoots, shorten its roots, and periodically repot it. Initially, you will need only branch cutters to shape it but, as your sculpture matures, you'll need other specialized tools to prune, form, and tweak it.

Clipping and cutting
To shape the tree, invest in a pair of branch cutters. Concave branch cutters are best for removing branches very close to the trunk, to avoid leaving a stump. They also

Keeping it together
A handy roll or belt (right) helps to keep track of all the tools needed for bonsai—from left to right, flat brushes, tweezers, three-pronged rake, leaf cutters, various pliers (also above right), and scissors.

Tools called Jin pliers are designed to strip bark to simulate the dead, bleached shoots caused by weather and lightning. You will also need a pair of pliers to manipulate the training wire, and long-handled wire cutters, with sharp, chunky jaws, which will bite through wire without harming bark or tissue.

Make sure you've got a good pair of scissors in your tool kit. Use a large-handled, thin-bladed pair to remove shoots, branches, and thin roots, and a long, thin-handled pair with narrow blades to cut off slender shoots and twigs sprouting from the crown of a tree.

Reminiscent of large tweezers with sheep-shearing blades, leaf cutters can also be used for removing soft, leafy shoots.

Tools for fine work

For plucking out young shoots or removing pests, such as caterpillars and greenfly, it is always very useful to have a good pair of tweezers handy.

For cleaning the soil, a flattened shaving brush with flexible bristles is ideal for sprucing up the surface and cleaning mud-splashed trays.

Separating matted roots when moving or resetting plants can be a tricky procedure. Short and stocky, with a tapered and grippable handle, the three-pronged rake is ideal for this task.

Shaping up

Actively manipulating the shape of a living tree requires some flexible tools. There's no better way of contorting a straight branch to make it look old and interesting than by binding it with one of several thicknesses of anodized aluminum wire.

You could also try the screw clamp. Comprised of two screw hooks, butterfly nuts, a metal bar, and a screw bolt with a clamp, it's invaluable for bending a branch or trunk without breaking it. With this gadget's help, you can simulate many fanciful shapes—arching or contorted, as from a river cliff.

To separate two closely spaced branches and improve a tree's shape, the best way is to push them apart with a length of wood with a V-shaped cut at each end.

In nature, lightning can tear a limb from the trunk. In bonsai, you can simulate natural wounds by gouging out lumps of bark with a very sharp wood chisel.

Potting your tree

The container should complement the tree it is holding. Trees with rounded crowns look best in oval pots. Pines, junipers, and azaleas all need very deep pots. Pines and junipers need unglazed pots, but most other plants do well in glazed ones.

Clamping its style

The tree clamp (above) manipulates the shape of stiff trunks and branches that do not respond to wiring. It has two hooks that can be adjusted to exert pressure on the tree.

help the cut heal more quickly and neatly than pruning shears. Knob cutters can also be used for taking off branches close to the trunk and removing trunk knobs and roots.

To trim off larger branches, a pull saw is the best tool to use. Cutting on the pull stroke reduces binding and improves the smoothness of the overall cut.

closely spaced plants. It has a lightweight frame, with two handles, like a bicycle, leading down to a single wheel with a pneumatic tire (filled with compressed air) to absorb impact.

Behind the wheel-hoe blade is a fitting for various interchangeable attachments like an oscillating head or a tined cultivator that will loosen the upper 4 inches of soil, disturbing any germinating weed seedlings. This is useful wherever plants grow in rows spaced widely enough for the user to pass without touching or damaging them, such as a larger vegetable patch. Any aeration value tends to be lost as the user walks behind the tool.

DRAW HOE
You can use the draw hoe with a pulling or chopping action to break up the soil. It is very effective at removing weeds and their roots, or for thinning seedlings. It has a flat blade attached to the shaft with a curved neck. To use it, stand beside the area being hoed and move either backward or forward. Turned upside down, the curved swan neck is useful for making a seed drill.

TRIANGULAR-HEADED HOE
You should use the triangular-headed hoe in a pulling action for making a shallow drill along a straight line, rather than for routine cultivations and weed removal.

Once the seeds have been sown in the drill, pull the soil gently back over them using the back of the blade. This less-common hoe does allow easy spot-weeding in the border and between closely planted seedlings.

DUTCH HOE
The Dutch or scuffle hoe is easy to use and has a sharp, angled blade at the leading edge of a D-shaped head. You can use it to cultivate the upper layer of soil by making short, sharp, push-pull strokes at a 20–30 degree angle and walking backward. This uproots small weed seedlings leaving them to wither on the surface or to be removed by hand for disposal.

Hoe, hoe, hoe
Modern hoes have evolved to suit local soil conditions and needs. Popular styles are the draw hoe (top), the triangular-headed hoe (center above), the Dutch hoe (center below), and the oscillating hoe (bottom).

OSCILLATING HOE

This is a double-action tool for removing weeds and loosening heavily compacted soil. It has a square-shaped head attached firmly to the shaft with a connection allowing it to rock back and forth in use. As both edges are sharp, this means that it can cut on the forward push and the backward pull, cutting weeds off below the soil's surface.

When should you hoe?

Hoeing is best when timed well. If the soil is too wet, you will create lumps, and the weeds will resist your attempts to remove them. Too dry, and the surface will be hard to break through—and doing so will allow moisture to evaporate. Aim to leave a finely broken soil texture that is clear of all weeds.

Once you have finished, clean any soil off the hoe and let it dry. Sharpen the blade with a file at least once a season to make sure it cuts easily as you work, and wipe it well with an oiled cloth.

RAKES

The rake is a gathering implement, used since Roman times for the harvest. They come in a variety of shapes and sizes, and may have a metal or wooden head. Early examples were made in a very practical fashion, with the teeth screwed into the head so that a broken one could be easily replaced. Even today, it is possible to find rakes with replaceable teeth, but they are more often cast as a single unit.

HOW TO USE THE RAKE

In the garden, you can use the rake for gathering stones, weeds, and hedge clippings. It is a vital tool for leveling and preparing a seedbed—but you should handle it lightly. Do not allow the teeth to dig in too deeply or you will spoil the effect by dragging large clods back to the surface. A combination of repeated raking and treading are the only means of producing the kind of seedbed essential for a new lawn.

Use it with a backward-forward, push-pull motion, bracing yourself as you bend forward and straighten. Try to work when the soil is moist, so that any lumps of soil will break apart easily. Avoid days that are too dry or wet as you will do more harm than good.

Losing a tooth
Old-fashioned cultivating rakes have individual teeth that are whittled from wood. Using the rake when soil is moist and workable will reduce the chance of a tooth falling out.

RAKE STYLE

The width of the rake can vary considerably, with the number of teeth on the head usually ranging from 10 to 16. The greater the number of teeth, the finer the soil surface will be after raking. The most common garden rake has a flat head and either flat or slightly curved tines. It will do for most tasks with the exception of major grading or landscaping, which will necessitate a proper wooden grading rake.

After use, wash and dry the rake thoroughly before storing. Wipe the head regularly with an oiled cloth to prevent rust, and check that no teeth are loose. Hang it in a dry place—preferably on the wall, for safety, so that the head cannot be accidentally stepped on.

CULTIVATORS

The traditional cultivator does not look much like a hoe, but plays a very similar role in the garden. It is designed to cultivate the upper layer of soil, break through surface compaction, and disturb weed seedlings. It usually has a long handle, and a head with between three and seven tines. Unlike the fork,

the tines are bent into sharply pointed hooks so that you can pull the tool through the soil in short, sharp movements like the draw hoe. The tines are flexible to absorb impact and staggered, like a clawed hand, so that you can make the equivalent of two pulls with just the one. Tine number, width, depth, and shape varies according to the intended use.

STYLES OF CULTIVATOR

There are many versions of the cultivator that vary distinctly from the traditional, straight-handled tool with three to seven tines. Some have short handles with a T-shaped top bar and plastic polypropylene hand grips. Others have four tines (like a fork) that are staggered, instead of flat.

Cultivators should be pushed vertically down into the soil with the sole of the foot and given a twist to loosen the soil to the depth of the tines. This tool is useful in a confined area, as it is operated from an upright position rather than at an angle. Use it to incorporate fertilizer, loosen weeds, aid water absorption, and reduce compaction. Where the plants are closely spaced, however, this type of cultivation may damage the roots by going too deep.

Dig deeply

Hook-like cultivators (left and above) break up the top layer of soil, relieving compaction, improving aeration, and allowing rainwater to filter down to the subsoil. These tools are especially useful in established borders.

For planting bulbs and annuals, weeding your borders, and transplanting rows of seedlings, a hand fork and trowel are indispensable. They are likely to be the tools that you use most often, so invest in good-quality products that will last for years to come.

HAND TOOLS

While the heavier work in the garden is done with long-handled tools, the more detailed, close-to work, such as weeding, tends to be finished off using hand tools—their smaller size allowing you to work nearer to the plants and without causing as much potential damage to the stems and roots of those plants that you are weeding around.

In the garden, close cultivation means getting down to ground level, and if you are working for any significant length of time, you will be kinder to your knees and back if you sit, rather than kneel or bend over as you work. It can be very therapeutic, on a warm summer's afternoon, to sit and work methodically through a border, just letting your mind wander where it will as you get rid of unwanted weed seedlings and dead leaves.

Basic tool kit

Like so many implements, there seems to be a huge variety of hand tools, but you will only need a basic trowel and fork to start off with. Depending upon the size of your garden, this may be all you'll ever need, but if you branch into growing vegetables you may find a use for specialty tools such as the onion hoe, which you may use for earthing up onions.

Joints

Although the less expensive tools are pressed and shaped from a single piece of metal, those with wooden (ash) handles usually have a tang-and-ferrule joint. The tang is a sharp, spear-like point at the top of the metal head that fits into the end of the shaft, and is clamped into place with a ferrule (a small ring of steel) to keep the wood from splitting. With a great deal of use, the tang will hit against the wood of the handle and create a space until it falls out. Generally, the more you pay for the tools, the better the ferrule will fit against the handle, and the longer the tool will last.

What to look for

Most hand trowels and forks show little variation in basic design, but vary considerably in terms of quality and cost. You should base your selection of any smaller hand tools on both sturdiness and comfort, as

Vegetable grower's tools

Eaten within a few hours of harvesting, home-grown vegetables are extremely good for you. Tasty and richer in vitamins than store-bought produce, they are worth a little extra effort and a few special tools.

Growing vegetables is easy. Simply stick to four basic rules: Site crops in full sun (they hate shade), rotate crops so that the big three (brassicas, root crops, and all other vegetables) are never on the same patch for more than one year in three, and enrich the soil with bulky manure and well-rotted garden compost. The fourth rule is to use the right tools for the job.

Planting vegetables

After preparing the ground, the first step to new life in the vegetable plot is sowing seed. By all means pinch seeds between your finger and thumb and trickle them into a seed drill, but for more precision, try a dispenser calibrated for six different sizes of seed. A dibber is one of the most useful tools for a

The point of the matter

Sow thinly using a seeder (far left) that has a suction bladder to pick up and place seeds, or one (left) that vibrates to shuffle the seeds off its tip. An asparagus knife (below left) cuts tough, new spears easily, and the soil cultivator (bottom left) saves work on your knees.

vegetable gardener. This slender cone of wood or metal, which may have depth indicators, is essential for planting cabbages, cauliflowers, brussels sprouts, kale, and leeks. When putting in brassicas, make a hole with a dibber and insert the roots and lower part of the stem. Firm in the plant by making a second hole next to the first and levering soil against the stem.

A garden line is necessary for marking rows when sowing or planting. This consists of two 21-inch lengths of metal, one of which has a rotating holder around which 45 feet of jute twine is wound or unwound. If the string gets wet, unwind and dry it, then rewind.

If you need something to stand on to sow or plant, you could use a board, but it's easier to unroll a path. Made from inter locking heavy-duty polypropylene slats, a portable path can stretch to any length you choose.

Protecting your crop

You may need a tunnel cloche to warm and dry soil to sow lettuce, carrots, turnips, and other crops in the spring. A strip of UV-proof

Protective measures

Polythene cloches (left) form a complete barrier retaining moisture and air, while creating a warm, humid environment.

polythene is draped over and secured to wire hoops, and can be erected quickly and easily. Some have built-in galvanized steel hoops to make a one-piece tunnel.

Ornamental and practical, a rhubarb forcing pot is a large, lidded pot made from terra cotta. Speed an early crop of tender pink stems by heaping leaves or straw over a dormant crown in winter. Enclose this with a forcing pot. Periodically, remove the lid to see how long shoots are. When they're just under the lid, remove the pot and enjoy eating the crop.

Harvesting vegetables

The asparagus knife is the tool for cropping fleshy spears. The new shoots, about 6 inches long, are cut 3 inches below the soil surface. You could sever them with a normal knife, but the asparagus knife, with its serrated blade, is ideal.

The long-handled draw hoe and the onion hoe will both come in handy. The former has a swan neck and a thin rectangular blade, the tip of which is angled to brush a taut garden line, to take out seed drills. Use it, too, for earthing-up trench celery and potatoes. The onion hoe is great to thin seedlings and weed around closely spaced crops. It is swan-necked with a wooden handle and a 3½-inch hemispherical blade.

the anatomy of a trowel

Choose a trowel that you find comfortable to hold, with a handle anchored firmly in place by a tang-and-ferrule design. The joint with the blade should also be strongly forged.

A deep dish and sharp blade lets you dig easily. Match the shape of the blade to the job in hand: if you are working in tight spaces or planting out seedlings and bulbs, a narrow and pointed blade will be helpful; for other digging tasks, a broader blade is preferable.

a smooth, well-made handle will reduce the risk of fatigue (caused by vibration as you work) and blisters. The handle may be made of ash (with or without a rubber handgrip), polypropylene, or aluminum (with head and handle cast as one unit). In some ranges, wooden handles are available in two lengths: 5 inches or 12 inches.

The head is usually metal, often carbon steel, although stainless-steel heads are available. A smooth surface on the blades or tines makes using and cleaning them much easier, so carbon steel models are often coated with rust- and scratch-resistant paint.

Small-scale hand tools

Short-handled tools include (left to right), the trowel, the hand fork, and the onion hoe. These are ideal for gardeners with a collection of containers or a few raised beds. The shorter the handle, the more precise your movements.

TROWELS

The trowel is used like a miniature spade or hoe in the garden, to dig small holes, transplant seedlings and small plants, turn over the surface of the soil, and loosen weeds. It has a short handle and a concave head with a rounded end, ideal for moving small quantities of soil, compost, or fertilizer around. A trowel enables you to work in a space as confined as a window box—where it is probably the only tool you will need until you branch out further.

Find a trowel best suited to your use. The more confined the space, or the smaller the plants you are handling, the narrower the trowel should be. After use, wash it thoroughly to remove any soil, and allow it to dry completely before putting it away. Wipe it regularly with an oiled cloth to prevent rust.

HAND FORKS

Just as the trowel is a miniature spade, so the hand fork is a small version of its much larger cousin, the border fork. A hand fork is useful for close-work in a border or container, particularly for breaking up the surface of the soil to allow rainwater to penetrate, for weeding and cultivating, and for mixing in a top-dressing of fertilizer.

The hand fork may have flat or round tines (the flat-tined designs are better for weeding), allowing access to confined spaces and closely established plants. Choose the hand fork that best suits your needs, in terms of hand size and material. However, there is no

point spending a lot of money on a stainless-steel hand fork if it is not a tool that you intend to use often. A stainless-steel tool, however, will last you a gardening lifetime.

ONION HOE

The onion hoe is a short-handled tool, designed like a small draw hoe. Use it in the vegetable garden for earthing-up (pulling soil up around the crop to blanch it or encourage growth) or pulling soil away to expose the crop to allow it to ripen, like the onion in late summer. Keep it low to the ground during use. It is small enough to use between closely planted crops, and can be used for weeding in a general way in flower borders and the vegetable plot.

THREE-PRONG CULTIVATOR

This scaled-down version of the long-handled cultivator allows you to aerate the soil in a confined or small area, such as a raised bed, where a full-sized implement won't work. The three curved or bent tines have pointed or flattened tips to scratch through the surface and loosen it.

>tools of the future

Don't damage your back doing hard work in the garden. Shop around for tools with comfortable handles that reduce the strain. There are more around each season and an increasing interest in our health means that this trend is likely to continue.

3

Controlling
the Environment

Watering wisely

Water is critical to the existence of plants. It's true that they need nutrients and light to thrive, but they need water just to survive. A plant may consist of as much as 90 percent water, which is responsible for all the plant's basic functions. Moisture around the roots allows nutrients and minerals in the soil to be absorbed, while within the plant, water keeps the cells firm and allows the movement of the starches and sugars needed for growth. Moisture also triggers the swelling of seeds and their germination.

Without water, a plant's activities are severely limited: Insufficient water can result in the shedding of buds, the premature drop of flowers, and poor color and size in the flowers that do open. It can also cause premature leaf loss or early fall color, the production of few or small fruits, and an increased susceptibility to attack from pests and diseases.

WHAT CAUSES WILTING?

A lack of moisture in the soil forces plants to use up the water supplies held within their tissues. Once the amount of water lost from the leaves exceeds that taken in by the roots, the plant will start to draw moisture from its own cells. As this happens, the cells shrink, each losing contact with its neighbor, resulting in the loss of stability that we see as wilting. Restoring the supply of moisture in time allows the cells to refill and the plant to recover. If the wilting goes too far, however, the cells cannot refill and the plant will die. The stage at which it is impossible to reclaim the plant is known as the "permanent wilting point."

When rainfall is low, a plant growing in the soil can send its roots deeper into the soil to find reserves of water trapped in the lower layers of subsoil. This is not the case, however, for plants that you are growing in containers. These don't have a reservoir of moisture that their roots can draw on, and therefore rely on you for their watering needs—which may become time-consuming.

Exactly how much water a plant requires depends on the type and size of plant, and the conditions around it. Water is lost from the plant through tiny pores on the underside of the leaf, in a process known as "transpiration." On a cool, calm day, transpiration

> ## "Gardening requires lots of water—most of it in the form of perspiration."
>
> ### LOU ERICKSON, CRITIC AND POET (1840–1921)

will be minimal, but on a windier day, moisture is constantly evaporating and being replaced from within the plant at a faster rate—so the plant's needs are greater. On a really warm, windy day, the loss is at its greatest, and the plant will use up a great deal of water. You may need to refresh container-grown plants twice on a hot day—particularly if they are leafy like tomato plants.

HUMIDITY AND WATER LOSS

The humidity of the air surrounding the plant also influences its rate of moisture loss. The more moisture there is in the air, the less water the plant will lose as the pressure within the leaf will be closer to that outside it. This applies particularly to house plants: The air indoors tends to be dry—especially in winter—when heaters and fires have a marked drying effect on the air.

The simplest method of increasing the humidity around a plant is to stand it on a wide saucer of pebbles and keep the saucer filled with water. The roots will have access to a constant supply of water without actually standing in it (and potentially rotting) and the water can evaporate around the leaves of the plant, reducing the moisture lost. Grouping your plants together also helps, as the canopy of leaves underneath creates a microclimate that raises the humidity level.

TIME TO WATER

Water your plants in the early morning and late evening, when the soil is cool and the atmosphere is relatively moist, as this will allow the maximum time for water to soak in before the heat of the next day. Watering when it's hot not only guarantees maximum evaporation, but also increases the danger of droplets on the leaves causing scorch.

Watering your plants can be extremely therapeutic, especially at the end of a stressful day when you can let your mind wander and your body relax. Through it you will get to know your plants and how much water each requires, while checking their health. If you are regularly away from home, however, you should try an automated watering system. It operates a timer and switches on at a specified time to deliver a preset quantity of water.

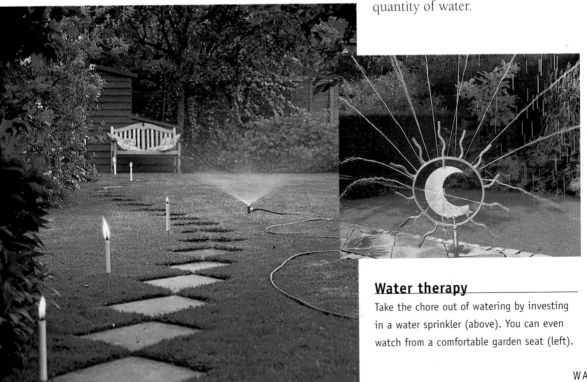

Water therapy

Take the chore out of watering by investing in a water sprinkler (above). You can even watch from a comfortable garden seat (left).

WATERING EQUIPMENT

Plants like to be treated gently. Drowning them in a strong jet of water will damage delicate leaves and stems, and also wash away valuable soil; on the other hand, too fine a mist may deprive the roots of sufficient moisture. Good-quality watering tools should therefore allow you to deliver a steady and controllable stream of water.

WATERING CANS

A good-quality watering can is a must for any gardener. You need it for spot-watering thirsty plants, moistening seed trays, and applying both liquid fertilizer and pesticide.

When buying a can for the first time, select a well-balanced one that is comfortable to carry when full and heavy. When filled, it should start to pour as soon as it is tilted. A can with a long spout will give you extra reach among the plants for individual watering. The volume of water the can will hold may be as little as a pint—which is useful for just a few house plants—and as much as 3½ gallons.

Look for a can with a detachable rose or nozzle that fits onto the spout. By changing the shape and size of the nozzle, you can be sure of delivering the correct amount of water to your plants. If you plan to raise seedlings, choose a nozzle that provides a spray of water rather than a jet. If you apply a jet to a small plant, you may wash it out of the soil and kill it, whereas a gentle shower will moisten it without harm.

Watering cans are generally made of plastic or galvanized steel. Plastic ones are cheaper, lighter, and will last many years providing they are protected;

> good ideas

If you never seem to have enough hands to carry everything you need around your garden, consider a watering can with side pockets for your hand tools. This model also has a domed half-lid to stop water from spilling out, and two handles that will help you tip the can when full.

inclement weather may cause them to degrade. Metal cans are more expensive and heavier, but will last indefinitely if cared for; rapid removal of any rust will prolong their life.

MISTERS

These are hand-held containers with a trigger that you squeeze to release a fine mist spray. They hold from

one to two pints of liquid and are ideal for increasing the humidity around smaller plants in the house or greenhouse. Buy a second and third mister to apply small amounts of foliar feed or pesticide—but keep these labeled and separate to avoid contamination.

Misters are small and inexpensive, made of plastic, and will last for many seasons. As with any plastic items, it is a good idea to store them out of direct sunlight to stop the material from degrading.

THE GARDEN HOSE

The hose will form the basis of your watering system once you progress beyond a single can. It takes the effort out of watering, saving you the back-breaking effort of carrying water from faucet to plants. The hose will deliver a constant stream of water and can be pulled around the garden to reach every plant.

When a lawn begins turning brown, it will take around 6 gallons per square yard to restore it. This volume is difficult to deliver without a hose, and in dry conditions it is more effective to soak the grass via a slow-running hose than to use a lawn sprinkler. The frequent light applications of water produced by a sprinkler encourage shallow rooting, making the grass vulnerable and less self-sufficient if watering is discontinued.

Hoses are made of vinyl, nylon, or polythene but they vary in quality, cost, and durability. The cheaper ones consist of a single layer of material; the more expensive ones have an inner tube coated in vinyl or a woven nylon mesh coated in vinyl (or a vinyl-rubber mixture). The latter are better for working at higher water pressures and are designed to resist kinking and degradation. Hoses are available in different colors, including green, brown, black, red, and sand, to blend or contrast with your garden.

Connectors These are useful for times when you need to join the hose to another item; if your garden is long, or the faucet in an inaccessible place, it may be necessary to join lengths of hose together. You may

THE LOWDOWN ON HOSING DOWN

You may think a hose is a simple piece of equipment, but in fact a lot of thought goes into making a good hose. Look for brands made from several different layers of material, which strengthen the hose and help to prevent kinking. To prolong the life of your hose, keep it properly coiled and out of direct sunlight (which will cause it to deteriorate).

wish to change from one type of watering device to another, such as the sprinkler to the hand pistol. Interchangeable fittings with snap-on couplings make this a convenient option.

Connectors are often made of brightly colored plastic that is easily visible in the garden, and each simply joins to the next by pushing together. Brass fittings offer a more permanent (although more expensive) system that will last a lifetime.

You can find fittings that will connect to the faucet (round or square), fit to the end of a hose ready to connect to another item, double the hose to feed two separate hoses, lengthen the hose by joining two together, and repair a split hose. They simply attach to the hose by a screw fitting, with rubber O-rings or circular springs to ensure a watertight fit.

Lances and pistols These are devices for delivering water and fit to the end of a hose with a connector. Pistols usually allow you to adjust the delivery from a fine spray to a direct jet, to suit the plants being watered, and include an on/off position for when you pause to examine a plant while watering. They can be plastic or brass (with a polypropylene grip). Lances come in brass or lighter-weight aluminum, with a molded grip, and provide an extension to the hose for reaching inaccessible plant containers, such as hanging baskets, to deliver a fine spray.

Watering nozzles

A round nozzle (left) delivers a gentle spray; long-handled extensions (middle) allow you to water out-of-reach containers and beds; oval nozzles (right) deliver a stronger spray, ideal for your more robust plants.

Fruit-growing tools

Sun-ripened apples and pears straight from the tree are a perk of growing fruit in your backyard. You can also enjoy the blossoms in the springtime and the many delicious desserts and pies you're able to make for next to nothing.

To make your fruit bush or tree more productive and to keep it within bounds, you will need to prune it. A conventional pair of pruning shears or loppers is usually adequate (see pages 69 71), but if you have weak wrists, use a ratchet, double-lever, or geared pruning shears and loppers that slice through shoots and branches easily.

Some apple varieties grow so fast each season that it is best to prune them with a pull-action saw designed to cut green, sappy wood without clogging. Choose a folding version with a high-carbon, hard chrome-plated blade with specially-set teeth that leave a knife-cut finish.

You'll need a pruning knife to pare ragged saw cuts and take off snags and side shoots (see page 77) and long-arm pruners will be invaluable for reaching shoots up to 15 feet from the ground. The last pruning tool you may need is a pair of vine scissors—ideal for snipping out shoots without damaging fruits; for thinning grapes; and spacing apple, pear and plum fruitlets.

Protecting your crop
Fruit cages are a good investment against bud-pecking and fruit-stealing birds. Don't stint on size, as you will regret it if you wish to

For delicate tasks

If you enjoy grafting fruit trees, a budding knife (left) will come in handy. Long and slender, with a serrated blade, vine scissors (below) are perfect for the fine work of thinning grapes.

For out-of-reach branches

A telescopic pole that you can fit with different heads, such as loppers (above) or a fruit picker (above right), is invaluable. When using a fruit picker, ease the metal "fingers" around a piece of fruit and give it a gentle tug to detach it.

increase your plantings in the future and have no room for them. A cage should also be 6–7 feet in height; it's no fun having to bend low to pick the fruit.

Essentially, a cage is made up of a galvanized or black plastic-coated steel frame draped with 1 inch mesh netting—usually made of polypropylene. You can use galvanized zinc wire for the sides of the cage but not the roof, as zinc

can dissolve in the rain and is toxic to plants. There should also be one or more doors with a "spade-end" hinge to prevent twisting.

Tree ties

Some trees, especially apples grafted onto dwarfing M27 rootstock, need support throughout their life. Do this by securing the trunk with an adjustable buckle tie, which prevents the bark from chafing, to a short stake pressure-treated with preservatives that keep it rot-free for many years.

Harvesting your fruit

The best part of a growing an apple, pear, or plum tree is eating the ripened fruit, but it has to be picked first. Be careful not to bruise the fruit.

If you can reach the fruit from the ground, or with a stepladder or

ladder tied to a branch, pack each gently, one by one, into a foam-lined bucket or wicker basket. Alternatively, place them in a canvas or strong nylon bag with handles; the best are both self-supporting and collapsible.

The finest fruits, however, are usually clustered on the ends of branches, often out of reach. The solution is to harvest the crop with a purpose-made fruit picker. Tools for picking fruit have a strong fabric bag attached to a crown of plastic, or galvanized prongs or fingers. Some have an adjustable angled head. Whichever you use, connect it to a lightweight, telescopic handle that allows you to pick fruits up to 17 feet from the ground. Simply maneuver the fruit stalk between the pair of prongs and tug gently. The fruit will drop into the bag. Gather one piece at a time to avoid bruising.

Nonreturn valves Fit a nonreturn valve onto your watering system between the electrical supply and the hose to prevent back-siphoning from contaminating the supply. This is particularly important if you add a liquid fertilizer to the water as you are applying it to the plants.

Hose reels Made of metal or polypropylene, a reel is a convenient device for keeping hoses neat, rather than unraveled and unsafe on the floor. You can carry it, mount it on the wall or wheel it around the garden, unwinding just the length of hose you need to reach the plant you want to water. Some models may have a guide that encourages the hose to run smoothly, and most have a winding handle or knob on the side to rewind the hose onto the central drum.

Hose guides and finials These protect border plants from possible damage as you drag the hose around the garden. Ornamental or retractable, each has a rotating reel on a vertical spike with which you anchor the guide into the ground. The retractable type is ideal for the lawn: Pull it up for use and push down again for easy mowing. Wall-mounted types prevent the hose from rubbing against the wall as it is used.

Diluters A through-hose diluter allows you to apply liquid fertilizer at the same time as watering. These relatively inexpensive devices release fertilizer into the water at an adjustable rate. They can be free-standing units for the larger garden, or smaller jug-shaped attachments near the hand grip. Each can be used with a lance or pistol-grip delivery system.

DRIP-FEED SYSTEMS

Using a hose can be a hit-and-miss affair unless you have perfected your technique. A more accurate system involves delivering water to individual plants, which reduces the amount of water lost by evaporation and weeds between the plants. There are two sorts of perforated hose to do this: One is flat with perforations on one side that send out a fine spray over a 2½-foot wide strip. The other is a rigid,

Lightening the burden

Make life easier for yourself by investing in a wall-mounted hose reel, which winds up automatically (left). Or, dispense with watering duties altogether and opt for an automatic drip-feed system (below).

circular hose with perforations around and along its length that allows water to seep out at a very low pressure directly into the soil.

Both perforated hoses are laid on the soil's surface and are good for irrigating large areas. The water soaks right down into the soil, encouraging plant roots to penetrate deeply. These pipes are often left in position permanently.

Both drip-feed systems can easily be automated, as the flow of water is slow and unlikely to overwhelm the plants. The timer may be electric or battery-driven, and can be set to deliver the water when it will be most beneficial to the plants, such as the late evening. It can be set to run every day of the summer or for short periods when you are on vacation. It is ideal if you work erratic hours or often forget to water. The run time is adjustable, from one minute to two hours, with a frequency from once an hour to once a week.

Container watering Spaghetti tubing consists of a main supply pipe, connected to fine pipes leading directly to each plant or container. These can be adjusted to deliver a steady, fine trickle of water, or drips, and are held in place on plastic clips. However, the fine gauge of the tubing means that this type of

system has a tendency to clog in water areas (with large amounts of free lime in the water), or if soluble plant foods are applied during watering.

SPRINKLERS
These fit onto the end of a hose and anchor into the ground, delivering a spray of droplets over a wide area. They are useful for watering a newly laid lawn to settle it in, but can be rather wasteful for any serious watering, as much of the water evaporates rather than penetrating down into the lower layers of the soil. This encourages shallow-rooting and makes the plants more susceptible to drought.

Static sprinklers These consist of a spike that you press into the ground and a nozzle that delivers the water in a circular pattern over a given area.

Rotary-hammer sprinklers Ideal for small areas, these are based on a nozzle and counterbalance mechanism that moves the water jet in a series of short, swinging motions.

Oscillating sprinklers These have a central spray bar with a series of holes in the top and sides. On the side of the bar is a drive mechanism, operated by water pressure, which moves the bar from side to side. The speed of oscillation is dependent on the water pressure. Many models are adjustable so the water covers different-sized areas.

Mobile sprinklers Connecting to the hose, these will travel over an area or planned route to water a larger area, such as a lawn. The front wheel follows the hose

Watering your lawn

Static sprinklers (left) deliver a circular pattern of water, ideal for small areas; rotary sprinklers (center) give larger coverage; oscillating ones (right) are perfect for rectangular and square lawns.

reel, and the rotation of the arms drives the forward momentum, so that the speed at which the sprinkler travels is dictated by the water pressure. The lower the pressure, the slower the speed.

Rotary sprinklers These have a number of nozzles on a central pivot that rotates in a circular motion. Water coverage is usually even, and the rotary speed is governed by the water pressure.

SPRAYERS

These may be hand-held, self-standing, or worn on the back during use. They are used chiefly to apply chemicals such as herbicides and pesticides, so if you garden organically, you may need one only for applying foliar feeds.

On manual types, you operate a pump handle that builds up the pressure inside the container in order to deliver the liquid. Control the rate of application by adjusting the delivery nozzle (which is usually at the end of a short lance) or the operating pressure of the carrying vessel. Remember to wash the sprayer thoroughly after each use, so that there is no chance of cross-contamination of chemicals.

A typical cordless, rechargeable, electric sprayer will give two hours continuous use from a single charge. Like the manual type, it has an adjustable nozzle, providing a cone or fan distribution pattern.

BUTTS

Use a water butt for short-term storage of water and collect rainwater via a gutter or drainpipe, as this will be much less alkaline than treated water. Most butts

>tools of the future

Watering a large area can mean that you are endlessly bending over to pick the hose up and move it around the garden with you. This innovative hose cart will put an end to tiring bending and also keep your hands clean: Pull the handle and the hose will be cleanly laid out, and push it to roll up the hose.

are fitted with a faucet and hose connector at the base so that you can fill your watering can. Cover the top of the water butt to exclude light and reduce the growth of algae in the water.

If you have a big garden or a vast vegetable patch, a large plastic barrel holding 40–50 gallons will be needed, though smaller barrels are available. A slim, rectangular, wall-mounted butt will fit tightly around the drainpipe and hold 25 gallons. A built-in diverter will prevent it overflowing.

Spraying trees

This used to involve either leaning precariously from a ladder, or reaching up from below and dodging the the falling spray. Now you can get a small, pressurized sprayer with a flexible hose extension that gives you an extra 8-foot reach. So, you can stand comfortably on the ladder and simply reach out over the tree.

Reading the weather

After you have been gardening for a while, you will begin to read the weather and recognize its changes. This knowledge will have an impact on what actions you take for the plants in your care. If the day is going to be hot, then the greenhouse needs to be ventilated and shaded, and your plants will need watering at least once. If it is going to be windy, taller plants might need protection, and in cold, wet conditions, you may have to move small seedlings indoors.

If you keep a record of the weather on a regular basis, you can look back and compare one year with another to see when plants flowered or cropped. This is not an arduous task, and can provide helpful insight.

WEATHER STATIONS

The most accurate readings are obtained when the instruments taking the measurements are in the ideal position. Your rain gauge should be outside so that it can catch the rain, and the wind-speed recorder should obviously be in an exposed position to catch the wind. But, the thermometer needs shelter from bright sunlight and hostile elements. The traditional weather station is a freestanding, four-sided box on legs, with louvered, rather than wood, sides. Few gardens today would have room for such a large case, but it is possible to buy or make a wall-mounted version with a screen front to house your thermometer.

RAIN GAUGES

Essentially a calibrated container, the rain gauge is designed to catch and measure a representative sample of the rainfall in your garden. Its accuracy depends on where it is positioned in the garden, and ideally it should be placed one foot above the ground and well away from overhanging obstructions such as trees, hedges, and buildings. It can also be used to measure the amount of water distributed by a lawn sprinkler, by positioning it on the grass about half way between the sprinkler unit and the outer edge of the watering pattern. Watering to a depth of half an inch twice a week (loamy soil) or three times a week (sandy soil) is adequate for good lawn growth.

All-in-one weather station
You can get a compact weather station (left) that stakes into the ground and monitors rainfall, wind speed and direction, and temperature. Most rain gauges measure rainfall in millimeters and inches (below).

SUNDIALS THROUGH THE AGES

Asundial is a device that measures the time. There are many different types, but most consist of a stationary stick or arm, known as a gnomon, that casts a shadow onto a plate or surface marked with the hours; as the sun moves through the sky, the shadow rotates across the plate.

The Egyptians used a form of sundial as early as 1500 B.C. This consisted of a tall stone obelisk that cast a shadow onto the ground; markers arranged on the ground indicated the time and identified the longest and shortest days of the year. Later, a more accurate sundial was developed, using the gnomon and plate system described above. Cultures as diverse as the Greeks, Romans, Arabs, and Chinese depended on these finely crafted instruments and different forms evolved, including horizontal, vertical, and tilted models. By the eighteenth century, however, clocks and watches began to supersede sundials, and today they are mostly prized for ornamental purposes.

The passage of the sun
Clockwise from top right: The ancient Egyptians measured time by looking at the shadow cast by an obelisk; a decorative vertical sundial; an armillary sphere—the arrow points polar north and casts a shadow on the equatorial band; a wall-mounted vertical sundial; a horizontal sundial of the sort commonly mounted on pedestals in gardens.

Rain gauges can be as simple as a calibrated funnel standing in a container. The less expensive ones may not be frostproof, and if a frost occurs while the container is holding water, then the resulting expansion will crack it. The newest ones are molded from styrene acrylonitrile, which is strong, clear, and durable. The gauges fit onto a broom handle driven vertically into the ground and have a scale on the side of the container for taking measurements. Readings should be taken daily and any water discarded.

WIND SPEED AND DIRECTION INDICATORS

To measure the speed and force of the wind, you need a small anemometer. This consists of three metal cups turned on their sides and fixed to a vertical spindle by arms that rotate when blown by the wind. The wind speed is calculated in knots from the number of rotations recorded on the meter during a certain period of time.

The direction of the wind can be registered using a wind vane mounted on a building or garden structure. This is a freely rotating, horizontal arm with a vertical, flat surface at one end and a pointer at the other. Knowing the prevailing direction will influence where you site certain structures in your garden and knowing the speeds will help you plan when to begin planting and whether to ventilate your greenhouse.

THERMOMETERS

Knowing the temperature around your plants allows you to decide when to ventilate, water, and protect them from frost. In the greenhouse, a sharp rise in temperature will cause stress to the plants, their rate of transpiration will increase, and the resultant loss of water may cause wilting.

Position your thermometer out of direct sunlight and the elements (rain, snow, and wind) so that the readout is representative of the general position; many thermometers are available for wall-mounting. Many give readings for both the maximum day temperature

Taking the temperature

Thermometers range from the traditional mercury types (left), to digital versions (center). Some models attach to the outside of a window frame (right), enabling you to take a reading without leaving the warmth of your home.

and the minimum night-time temperature, so that you can see if a frost is coming and the plants need protection. Garden thermometers give readings in both Celsius and Fahrenheit, and will last many years as long as they are not damaged.

HYGROMETERS

These devices measure the humidity of the atmosphere. In many cases, a digital thermometer will give a humidity reading as well, which allows you to decide whether the moisture levels in the air around your plants are adequate. You can then decide whether you need to dampen the floor to increase the humidity level, or ventilate to lower it. Traditional hygrometers operate using human hair (or a synthetic replacement for it) on a hair-spring movement.

BAROMETERS

Changes in the weather are heralded by a change in atmospheric pressure. A barometer will record these changes and give you advance warning of what is to come. A steady rise in pressure usually indicates good weather to come, and a rapid fall, bad. There are two types of barometer, mercury and aneroid (or dry). The latter are portable and cheaper.

Greenhouse tools

Conservatories and greenhouses are apt to get very hot in the summer and cold in the winter, so you will probably need to take steps to create a balanced growing environment for your plants.

RESERVOIRS

A mains reservoir will stabilize the flow of water for a drip-feed system, steadying and reducing it to provide a continuous supply at a suitable rate. A plastic case and aluminum lid make it ideal for the greenhouse.

A 1 quart capacity plastic water reservoir can be attached to the side or end of the benching in the greenhouse. It has an aluminum lid to exclude light and prevent the growth of algae, and will hold enough water to supply capillary matting laid along the bench to keep the plants standing on it moist. The automated version is connected to a water supply and has a ball valve to start and stop the flow. The supply may be the mains, a water butt, or an overhead tank.

CAPILLARY MATTING

This is a coarse, loosely-woven, cotton-polyester material designed to allow free movement of water over a flat, level surface. Use it to cover your bench before laying your pots out, and it will act as a wick, drawing water from a reservoir for distribution to the plants. Ensure good contact between the matting and the compost in the pot, so the water can be sucked up by the capillary action of the compost and used by the roots. If the pots have been "crocked" with pieces of broken terra cotta, the system won't work.

Adequate ventilation

Introduce a much-needed breeze to the greenhouse during the hot summer months with adjustable slats (right), which you open by hand, or install automatic vent openers (far right).

SELF-WATERING TRAYS

Each consists of a watertight plastic base tray (the reservoir) and an aluminum insert that holds a layer of capillary matting. The matting draws water up from the reservoir for the plants. There should be enough water for two weeks' supply—while you are away on vacation, for instance. They are available in a wide range of sizes and colors.

GREENHOUSE SHADING

In summer, the heat inside the greenhouse, especially at midday, can be intense. This will increase the rate of transpiration of the plants, leading to wilting, and more directly, it can scorch the leaves by literally cooking the cells on the leaf surface.

You can buy blinds that you attach to either side of the greenhouse windows. External woven plastic ones are supplied on a roll with a pulley bracket and strong nylon thread to allow them to be pulled up or down. They will give partial or total coverage, according to weather conditions, and will last for many years,

Heating and cooling

A portable electric fan heater (far left) is one of the easiest ways to keep your greenhouse warm during winter. If you prefer not to install blinds in the summer, reduce and diffuse the sunlight by painting whitewash or diluted emulsion onto the outside of the glass or plastic (left).

especially if you store them indoors over winter. Woven green shade netting can be used inside or out, and has a four- to five-year life expectancy. Its pre-woven slits allow you to anchor it to the roof.

Inside the greenhouse, polyester roller blinds with nonrust aluminum rollers will last at least five years. The same fabric, bought loose, can be laid in the roof supports of a larger greenhouse and drawn across as required. Dot matrix shading film is self-adhesive (by static electricity) to flat glass or polycarbonate panels, although it will not stick to heavy corrugations. It may also be used outside, but will not last as long.

INSULATION

During winter, you can greatly reduce the amount of heat lost from inside your greenhouse by insulating it. This helps to keep the greenhouse frost-free and allows you to sustain plants without the cost of a heater. The simplest form of insulation is bubble polythene, which has two layers of clear polythene welded together into layers of bubbles, producing a triple-glazed effect. You can buy it on a roll, cut it to length, and attach it to the inside of your greenhouse frame with plastic clips. Remove and store it once the danger of frost has passed.

HEATERS

The two main benefits of greenhouse heating are that you can keep tender plants alive in winter and sow seed for new plants early in the season. These new plants will be ready to go outside as soon as the weather warms up. You have several options:

Electric heaters With variable thermostatic controls, electric fan heaters can be used without heat as fans during the summer to circulate air and cool the greenhouse. They can be freestanding or wall-mounted. Hot air blowers can be freestanding or hung from the roof. Air is drawn over an electric-powered, heating element. Designed for wall-mounting, electric convector heaters operate almost silently. Position them so that air can flow freely through both top and bottom.

Gas heaters The fuel can be propane or natural gas. Their thermostats may incorporate a safety cut-out carbon dioxide sensor that operates when the level of oxygen falls too low for healthy plant growth.

Paraffin heaters These range from very small heaters intended to keep the temperature barely above freezing to larger ones that can maintain a much higher temperature or heat a larger space. They are cheap to run and give off small amounts of carbon dioxide, which is used by the plants to grow.

AUTOMATIC VENT OPENERS

Ideally, a greenhouse should have a ventilation area equal to a fifth of the floor area, and this should include louvered vents in the sides, as well as opening roof panels. Automatic vent openers (for the roof or side panels) are ideal if you are out during the day or are unable to act if the temperature rises quickly. They operate using an enclosed cylinder of wax, which expands with heat to push a piston, which in turn causes the vent to open. As the wax cools, it contracts and a spring closes the vent again. You can preset the temperature at which they open to suit your plants. Some have a hydraulic damper to prevent the window from twisting if caught by a strong gust of wind.

4

Cutting
and Trimming

Lawn care

The lawn is an essential part of most gardens, providing a counterpoint to colorful borders. It acts much like the carpet does indoors, linking areas together throughout the garden and providing soft paths underfoot. You can use it as a soft surface on which to play games or to simply sit on to enjoy the sights and sounds of the garden. However, if you want to keep it in good condition (which requires hard work) it will occupy as much time in maintenance as any other aspect of your garden.

You can adapt the level of maintenance to suit the situation, because not everyone wants the same from their lawn or wants to put in the same effort. A beautiful, fine-leaved lawn with mowing stripes will look perfect in an ornamental situation where there is little or no foot traffic, but where there are children, the grass will need to be much tougher to withstand a wide range of activities. If a wildflower meadow is your preferred option, you will need to cut the lawn once or twice a year to coincide with the flowering frequency of the plants growing through the grass.

Ornamental gardens

To keep a high-quality, formal lawn looking its best, use a cylinder mower with a roller, which will give the finest cut and create a banded effect (main picture). You will probably want to tidy up the edges of your borders with a half-moon edging iron (inset).

Mowing is one of the routine, necessary tasks of gardening that makes all the difference to the health and appearance of your garden. While it is actively growing, your lawn may need mowing once a week to keep it looking good. But, the benefits are not confined simply to shortening the length of the individual grass blades; by cutting and rolling them, you are encouraging the plant to "tiller," or shoot again from the base. This results in a short, bushy plant which can withstand being walked on, rather than a single-leaved one that, if damaged, will die and leave a bare patch.

Lawns are seldom made up of a single species of grass, as the finer ones that give the best-looking finish are not hardwearing underfoot and benefit from the presence of tougher varieties to protect them. Though, if the lawn is not cut regularly, the stronger species will dominate the finer ones, resulting in a much coarser and more uneven finish.

CUTTING TIPS

Mowing is best undertaken when the grass is dry, so that the clippings will be light and easy to deal with. Cutting wet grass will clog the mower blades—causing you to have to stop and clear them—and also risks ripping the entire grass plant out of the soil. Allow the lawn to dry for at least 24 hours after heavy rain, until the ground beneath is not too wet. Morning dew can be swept off with a broom or a length of hose to dry the lawn more quickly.

The golden rule of mowing is that you never remove more than one third of the total height of the grass in a single cut. Thus, set the blades high for the first cut of the year in the spring, and then reduce them in height as the season progresses.

SAFETY PRECAUTIONS FOR ALL MOWERS

- Use a ground fault circuit interrupter (see page 128) for all mowers powered by electricity.
- Unplug before you make any adjustments.
- Never leave the machine with the motor running.
- Make sure the blades are securely attached.
- Wear sturdy footwear and pants in case the mower goes over your foot or flicks out a stone.

LAWN MOWERS

So many mowers are now available that the hardest part of maintaining a lawn can often be deciding which mower to buy! For optimum efficiency, choose a mower that suits the size and style of your lawn. If you have a large lawn, for example, invest in a machine with a wide blade; for those with smaller grassy areas, a mower with narrow blades will be more suitable. If your lawn has tight curves or corners, a smaller model will be easier to maneuver.

MOWER POWER

One of the first things you need to consider is how you wish to power your mower. There are four main options from which to choose.

Manual mowers are propelled by you. Cheap, quiet, and with no awkward cords, these also provide a great aerobic workout for you! They are eco-friendly but

hard work to operate, particularly on slopes, so are probably most suitable for small lawns. They don't cope well with very long or wet grass. Some hand-push models have wheels at the sides, but these make it difficult to mow right up to the edges. Others are operated with a chain from a heavy roller at the back; this type of mower is easier to mow over edges, and also creates attractive stripes on your lawn.

Electric-powered mowers are easier on the muscles, but their range is limited by the length of the cord. They tend to overheat when used for long grass and tough jobs, and for safety reasons should never be used on wet grass. If your lawn is very large or situated away from your home (and thus the power supply), these may not be the best option for you.

Gas-driven mowers are the most powerful type, but also the most expensive and difficult to maintain. They are the best choice for large gardens as they can cover ground quickly, and you don't have to worry about trailing cords. Opt for one with an electric ignition for ultimate ease of use: The pull-start models can be difficult to get going.

WHICH MOWER IS RIGHT FOR YOU?

	CYLINDER	ROTARY	RECIPROCATING KNIFE	FLAIL	NYLON-CORD TRIMMER	
Rough grass/scrub			O	O	O	
Uneven ground		O	O		O	
Long grass		O	O	O		
Awkward space					O	
Short grass	O	O	O			
Ornamental	O	O				

The rotary mower

Ideal for family lawns, rotary mowers are
generally fitted with rear-mounted grass bags
or boxes. The blade (inset) revolves at high
speed, a bit like a helicopter, cutting
through the grass as it goes.

Battery-powered mowers are not sufficiently
powerful to tackle large gardens without needing to be
recharged, but they are perfectly suitable for small and
medium-sized gardens.

THE CUTTING EDGE

The next choice you need to make concerns the way
the mower actually cuts the grass. First consider the
type of lawn you have in your garden. Is it purely
ornamental, or will the children be playing on it? The
more ornamental the lawn, the finer the finish you
will need from the mower, so you should be looking
for one with a cutting cylinder rather than a rotary
blade. Check that the handle is at the right height for
you and that the weight suits you before you make a
purchase. Bear in mind also that a good mower will
last for years if you maintain it properly, so buy what
you may need in ten years time, as well as what suits
your needs today.

>tools of the future

Mowing even a small lawn can be a chore, which is why
some ingenious manufacturers have developed robotic lawn
mowers that do all the work for you. The only preparation
necessary is to install a sensor cable around the edge of the
lawn. Then you simply press the "on" switch and the mower
will navigate its own way around the grass. When the
machine approaches the cable, impact sensors redirect it.
These sensors also keep the mower away from hard
obstacles. There is no grass box, but regular trimming
ensures that cuttings fall, die, and fertilize the lawn.

Some models are solar-powered, while others have a
battery that supplies the current. The latter come with a
special charging station in which the computer senses when
the battery needs recharging, and a guide wire directs the
machine back to the charging station.

THE HISTORY OF LAWN MOWERS

Plans for the first lawn mower were patented in 1830 by an English engineer named Edwin Beard Budding. His machine consisted of a large rear roller and a front cutting cylinder, with gear wheels that transferred power from the roller to the cylinder. Over the next few decades, lighter, quieter machines were invented that used a chain or side wheels to drive the cylinder.

Steam and the more popular gas-powered mowers were being manufactured at the end of the nineteenth century, and in the 1920s and 1930s, electric and rotary cutting machines started to appear. The basic design of the domestic mower then changed remarkably little for years, until the hover mower was born in the early 1960s.

Taking care of the lawn

Counterclockwise from top: a nineteenth-century cylinder mower with a front-mounted grass collection box; the well-manicured lawn became an achievable dream in the 1950s and 1960s, thanks to cheaper and more efficient mowers; gas, electric-, and battery-powered machines made mowing even easier; the lightweight hover mower caught on quickly in the 1970s; today's ride-on models require little effort.

Some mowers leave the cut grass on the lawn; others come equipped with bags or boxes for collecting the clippings; and some actually recycle the clippings as they mow, cutting them down to a fine mulch that is then left on the lawn to decompose and return nutrients to the grass.

Cylinder mowers Manual or powered, these give the best results, especially when cutting the finer grass species. They work thanks to their metal blades, arranged in a spiral on a cylinder, which brush very closely against a fixed blade and cut the grass in a scissor action. The number of blades varies from three to twelve—the greater the number, the finer the cut.

These mowers generally have a large rear roller, which flattens the grass and encourages "tillering" (more shoots growing from the base of the plant), and a small front roller, which supports the front and allows you to adjust the cutting height.

After use, clean any clippings off the blades of the cylinder and wipe them clean with an oiled cloth. Store the mower in a dry place. With average use, the blades will probably need sharpening every two years, but they can be tested by feeding a piece of newspaper between the blade and the sole plate.

Hand mowers The traditional hand-powered push mower makes the sound so readily associated with the warm, sunny Sunday afternoons of childhood. It was a much less intrusive noise than the irritating, nonstop drone of today's electric models that invades the consciousness like the buzzing of a nearby wasp. The

Mower details

A height adjuster for the blades (left) allows you to control the cutting height. Rollers (center) create a striped finish. The safety handle (right) will cut out the engine if you let go of the handle.

hand mower is ideal for small lawns, an excellent form of exercise, and totally environmentally friendly.

This type of cylinder mower is usually fitted with a large, heavy, rear roller, which provides the drive for the machine via a chain or gear connection to the front cutting cylinder. In the hands of an experienced user it gives a wonderful striped effect.

Smaller models, often called reel mowers, are quick and easy to use, with just a cutting cylinder and driven by two side wheels, with or without a grass box to collect the cuttings.

Rotary mowers These are usually electric or gas-powered. They have horizontally-set blades which rotate at high speed—around 3000 rpm—cutting as they spin. The number of blades varies from machine to machine, between two and four, and they may be triangular or rectangular.

The finish is not as good as that of the cylinder mower, but is ideal for play areas and "useful" lawns. As the season progresses, you can vary the height of cut. Set the cutting height high at the beginning of the season, and then lower it as desired to produce shorter grass for a neater finish, or longer for greater tolerance

You can move the hover sideways as well as backward and forward, making it a good choice for gardens with awkward turns, banks and slopes, and overhanging plants.

Hover mowers This type of rotary mower operates on a cushion of air without the need for wheels. A fan mounted on the engine draws air in through holes in the top of the cover, forcing it down to create the pressure that lifts the machine. Having no wheels makes this very maneuverable on steep slopes and uneven areas, and for cutting long or wet grass.

After use, remove any clippings which are stuck in the intake grill or on the blades and wipe clean with an oiled cloth. Store the mower in a dry place. With average use, the blades will probably need sharpening or replacing every one to two years.

Ride-on mowers These are invaluable for very big gardens. They move faster than you could walk and have an extra-wide cutting width that makes quick work of even the largest lawns. They are not, however, suitable for fine lawns.

Reciprocating knife mowers Best suited to long grass and light scrub, these have been almost superseded by the trimmer. They have two toothed bars set one above the other. As the upper "cutter" bar moves out and back across the lower one, the grass is trapped between the blades and cut. This type of mower is usually engine-driven and self-propelled.

to drought. This adjustment is made by raising and lowering the wheels, moving the rotating disk assembly up and down, or using spacers between the motor and the rotating disk.

Keep the blades sharp and free of dried grass so that they cut properly, and replace them if they are damaged by hitting a stone or other obstruction. After use, clean any grass off the blades and wipe them clean with an oiled cloth. With average use, the blades will need sharpening or replacing every two years.

The two extremes
The simplest mower is the reel mower (far left), which is best suited for small lawns; ride-on mowers are expensive, but take the hard work out of cutting a large expanse of lawn.

Reciprocating knife mower

If you have large, overgrown areas in your garden, this machine will efficiently tackle heavy undergrowth or scrubby grass.

The power source can be either gas, electricity, or battery. They typically have a cutting diameter of about 9 inches, a cord length of 40 feet, an alloy shaft, and a polypropylene hand grip. The hand grip may rotate to make working at an angle easier, and the nylon cord may be manual- or tap-fed.

If your trimmer has an electric cord, always keep it over one shoulder so you can't cut through it, and use a ground fault circuit interrupter (see page 128).

Flail mowers These are useful for coarse grass or areas of light scrub, and can deal with grass up to 3 feet high, although they are losing ground today to the trimmer. The mower incorporates a horizontal rotor carrying a number of swinging metal flails turning at high speed. Each flail has a cutting edge and is held in its cutting position by centrifugal force.

Nylon-cord trimmers These are really rotary scythes, with nylon cord feeding out from a spool and rotating at high speed. They are ideal for trimming weeds and grass in inaccessible areas. Their great attraction is that the nylon cord does not damage brickwork, so you can trim right up to the base of a wall or the edge of a path, where the mower will not cut. They will also cut around trees and gate posts—in fact, almost anything which usually gets in the way of a mower.

Trimming your garden

For awkward, hard-to-reach spots such as around trees, under over-hanging plants and hedges, and next to walls and fences, a trimmer should be your choice of tool. The nylon cord (inset) revolves at high speed, cutting as it turns. As the cord wears away, more can be fed out to replace it.

"Nothing is more pleasant to the eye than green grass kept finely shorn."

FRANCIS BACON, PHILOSOPHER AND ESSAYIST (1561–1626)

HAND TOOLS

These add the finishing touch once the mechanized tools have done the bulk of the work. Their smaller size allows you to work in confined spaces and tidy up anything the larger tools have left behind. As you work, you can also check the health of the plants and the lawn to see if any remedial action needs to be taken.

SHEARS

The manual alternative to the powered trimmer in inaccessible areas is a pair of lawn shears. They closely resemble their hedging counterparts, but with the addition of long handles so you can work standing upright with blades set at an angle. Comfort grips and shock absorbers on the handles make them easy to use, and the blades often have a nonstick coating to help them cut more easily and resist sap. If you have only a small area of rough grass to cut—or just want

For awkward corners of lawn

Tidy up areas around trees and other obstacles that aren't tackled by your mower with a pair of long-handled lawn shears.

to trim long grass straggling from the lawn into the border—these are an economic alternative to the mechanical variety. Some models have telescopic handles so they can be adjusted to the most comfortable working length.

Small, single-handed shears are sometimes sold as grass shears, and will cut in even the most restricted areas. They have scissor-like blades which swivel through 180 degrees so you can use them horizontally, vertically, or at an angle, and left- or right-handed.

EDGING TOOLS

There are two main edging tools: edging shears and edging irons. The former are used to emphasize the boundary of a lawn. They have scissor-like blades set at 90 degrees to the long handles, so that you can work upright and sideways along the edge of the lawn to the left or right. Use them to finish off the lawn after mowing, neaten all the edges, and you can even buy shears that catch the cuttings. A battery-powered version with two rows of toughened, steel blades can be used kneeling or standing (with a telescopic extension handle).

the anatomy of **shears**

Look for smooth handles of wood (ash is a popular choice) or polypropylene for a lighter-weight option. Specialist lawn shears are available with long handles, which enable you to work from a standing position. Some models have ergonomically designed handles: try them out to make sure they suit you.

Stainless steel or carbon steel are the best materials for the blades. Shock absorbers (usually in the form of rubber stoppers) at the base of the blades will take the strain from your wrists.

Finishing touches

Grass shears (far left) are useful for small patches of grass and for cutting areas out of the reach of the mower. Border shears (left) make easy work of tidying the edge of the lawn, once you have finished mowing.

The edging iron (or half-moon) is an alternative to shears, with a sharp, semicircular blade mounted on a spade handle. Use it to recut an uneven or crumbling lawn edge by driving it down vertically with the foot to separate the unwanted edge. You may only need it three or four times during the growing season, whereas the edging shears may be used every 14 days when the grass is growing vigorously.

GRUBBERS

These are small, hand-held tools for removing individual daisies and other weeds from the lawn causing as little disturbance as possible to the surrounding grass, or for weeding in difficult places like the cracks between paving. The so-called "weed grubber" has a short, narrow blade with a V-cut end on a metal shaft, and the "daisy grubber" has two short prongs on a long, narrow blade.

Both are mounted into the (usually) wooden handle with a tang-and-ferrule, and are used by driving them down into the ground immediately next to the

Weeding your lawn

To root out individual weeds such as daisies and dandelions, use a daisy grubber. The forked blade enables you to work underneath deep taproots so that you can be sure of removing the whole plant.

offending weed. Use leverage gently to bring out the roots of the plant without taking too much soil or surrounding grass as well. The blade of the daisy grubber may be angled for easier use.

AERATORS

If your lawn has become compacted from too much water or from being walked on, you need to loosen the soil again. The easiest way to do this is to use an aerator. These range from a simple pair of shoes with spikes on the underside that you use to walk over the

If your lawn is a large one, an electric aerator will come in handy. As you push it across the grass, the spikes at the bottom penetrate the ground, enabling air, water, and nutrients to reach the roots more easily.

lawn, to large machines with hollow, solid, or flat tines mounted on a drum that is pushed or propelled over the lawn. Although solid tines open up vertical channels in the lawn through which air can enter, the area between holes is compacted even more to create them. By removing plugs of soil (which can be used as top-dressing when they have dried), you can fill the holes with quick-draining sharp sand. This will speed up drainage and open up the soil generally, as the organisms within the soil mix the sand in.

The manual aerator has a spade-like handle of wood or metal (or two straight handles with a cross piece at the top), and two to four tines on a horizontal bar that you push vertically into the ground with your foot and pull up again. The tines should be about 6 inches long to be fully effective and should penetrate the compacted layer of soil about 4 inches below the surface.

SCARIFIERS
The term "scarifying" is given to the removal of dead material or thatch from a lawn where it accumulates at

Condition your lawn
When the roots are properly nourished, the grass will look thicker and greener. Scarifiers range from compact manual models, which are suitable for small lawns, to large heavy-duty electric or gas-driven machines.

the base of the grass plants. If you do not remove thatch regularly, it builds up to the extent that the grass starts to root into the thatch rather than the soil beneath, making your lawn weak and susceptible to drought and fungal attack. Scarifying your lawn every month or two encourages the growth of stronger, healthier grass.

If you have a large expanse of lawn, use a mechanical scarifier with a spiked drum that combs the thatch out. Ideally the scarifying tines should be set so that they penetrate to the soil's surface. For the smaller plot, however, a hand-operated version is perfectly adequate. This consists of a metal head with about 24 tines on a straight bar that is attached to a long, wooden handle. It resembles a flexible rake but has stronger tines.

FLEXIBLE RAKES
The fan rake (sometimes known as a "springbok") can also be used for removing thatch from the lawn, as well as any moss or dead leaves in the fall. It has fine, circular, wire-like, metal tines in a fan shape, curved

Fallen leaves not only spoil the appearance of an otherwise pristine lawn, but can also encourage diseases and yellowing if left to decompose. A springy plastic lawn rake will allow you to quickly skim leaves and other debris from the surface of the grass before they can do any damage.

ROLLERS

These are intended to flatten any bumps in the lawn and encourage tillering, but are heavy and seldom needed on the average lawn, as their weight can cause soil compaction. The roller of a cylinder mower is just as good for its tillering effect, while imperfections can be cured by lifting and re-laying horizontally a small area of turf.

toward their ends and held in place against a sturdy metal frame. Adjust the tines to increase or reduce the width of the fan, depending on the space available. The rake will comb through the grass, snagging any debris and pulling it out as it goes. Bamboo and plastic versions are also available. (See pages 31 and 98–99 for more information on rakes.)

TURFING IRONS

Used for lifting turf which is to be relaid, the turfing iron is designed to slide underneath the grass, lifting the plants and the soil in which their roots grow. It has a flat, heart-shaped, carbon-steel head on an angled shaft, which in turn attaches to a wooden, spade-type handle. Choose a point about one inch below the soil surface and use short pushing strokes to slide the iron horizontally beneath the turf.

Smooth out the bumps

Lumps and bumps can turn into unsightly bare patches after mowing, which is why some gardeners like to use a roller. Traditionally, lawn rollers were very heavy iron implements. Today, most models consist of a hollow reinforced plastic drum, which you fill with water to add weight.

Pruning and cutting tools

In the garden, you will regularly find you need to trim something or other. It may be as small as a stray shoot or dead flower, but now and again, it will be larger, such as removing an overhanging branch for safety reasons. Always bear in mind that the right tool for the job makes the task in hand much easier.

The equipment needed for this task can vary considerably from small and lightweight tools to large, heavy-duty, professional ones. Every gardener needs a good pair of pruning shears, as they are so versatile, but not everyone needs something as large as a chain saw. Tools like this, unless you have a very large plot, are best rented as and when you need them.

The other tools in this category will find their way into your collection as your interest in gardening develops. Venturing into fruit-growing, for instance, may well mean investing in long-handled pruners. Taking up propagating your own plants will mean getting at least one good knife, and planting a hedge will necessitate buying shears or hedge trimmers. Renting is a good means of trying out different tools before you buy to see if you really do need your own, and if so, which are the right ones for you.

Your choice of cutting tools will be governed by the plants you are growing, although a good pair of pruning shears are a necessity for any gardener. If your heavy pruning is a once-a-year blitz, then it is worth considering renting the equipment, rather than housing it unused for the other eleven months. If you buy your own, look for a good brand, as cheaper tools are more likely to break as you use them, causing damage to the plant, you, or both.

Cutting tools are designed to cut—an obvious statement, and must be kept sharp. They should be stored in a dry, frost-free place, cleaned thoroughly after each use, wiped regularly with an oiled cloth to prevent rust, and taken for professional sharpening every one to three years, depending on how often they are used. See Chapter 9 for more information on maintaining your cutting tools.

Bypass pruning shears

The curved blades hold the stem in place and make a clean cut, helping to protect the plant from pests and disease.

PRUNING SHEARS

You can't beat a good pair of sharp pruning shears for most types of pruning. They are as essential to the gardener as the plants themselves, and once you find a pair that fits your hands, you will use them for years. They are intended for light pruning of woody plants, but most can cut through shoots up to finger thickness: You will need loppers to cut anything bigger than this. Pruning shears are also useful for deadheading, cutting flowers for indoors, and

Anvil pruning shears

The sharp upper blade cuts down onto a softer flat anvil, slicing through the branch or stem. The cut is slightly stronger than that of bypass pruning shears, making them ideal for hard, woody growth.

problem—even in a tight corner if necessary; and check that you can easily operate the safety lock, which keeps the blades closed when not in use.

CHOOSING THE RIGHT PRUNING SHEARS

Most are made of carbon steel, and the blades may be coated with a nonstick material to make cutting easier and reduce the chance of sap hurting them. The hand

preparing cuttings for propagation. They should not be used for cutting wire (which will damage the blade) or ripping into bags of compost (which may get into the mechanism).

Really good pruning shears will be expensive, but they are a good investment. If you spend as much as you can afford, they will repay you by lasting a lifetime, with just a little regular care. Do try them out before you buy to ensure comfort and ease of use. Most manufacturers make both right- and left-handed pruning shears, and some with an ambidextrous grip and thumb catch. Look for a brand with replaceable blades, too.

When trying them out, test the weight in your hand; try extending the handles (are they too wide for you?); ensure you can open and close the blades with no

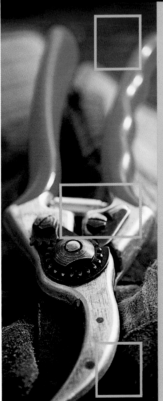

the anatomy of pruning shears

Handles should be molded with a nonslip grip, allowing you to easily maneuver among the branches of your plants.

The safety lock should be well positioned for maximum ease of use, and simply operated with the flick of your thumb.

Blades should be replaceable and may be coated with a nonstick finish to prevent rust and reduce friction. Some models have a sap groove in the blade.

grips are generally fiberglass, molded nylon, or lightweight aluminum alloy coated in molded vinyl to ensure they don't slip while cutting. Look for a shock-absorber between the handles, which prevent injury to your fingers.

You will find several different types of pruning shears in your local garden store:

Bypass (or parrot-bill) pruning shears have two curved blades that bypass one another very closely and cut in a scissor-like action. This most popular type of pruning shears is ideal for your more delicate plants as the cut is very precise.

Anvil pruning shears chop like a knife, with a single straight-edged cutting blade that closes down onto a flat bar of metal (often brass) called an anvil. These are not quite as easy to maneuver between tight branches as their bypass cousins and can also slightly crush the stems as they cut, but they are better at tackling hard woody stems.

Blade and half-anvil pruning shears have one convex cutting blade that cuts past a second, fixed, curved bar, in a bypass cutting action.

Manaresi pruning shears have two blades, both with straight cutting edges, which meet as the cutting action is completed. These are often preferred for pruning vines.

Ratchet-action anvil pruning shears have a special mechanism (the ratchet) that enables you to cut through a branch in stages. Each time you squeeze the handle, the blade works deeper into the stem, until it has cut right through. These help to reduce fatigue, and are ideal for gardeners with smaller hands, although the cutting action is slower than that of conventional models.

HOW TO USE PRUNING SHEARS
Always position the stem to be cut close to the base of the blade where it can be held firmly. If the cut is made with the tip, the blades are likely to be strained or forced apart. Always make a clean, straight cut—don't twist the pruning shears or your wrist. If you can't cut through cleanly, the stem may be too thick, and you may need to use loppers instead.

Each type of pruning shears can produce a good, clean cut if used correctly and provided it is kept clean, sharp, and in good condition.

Pruning a shrub or ground cover rose

1 If you are pruning a rose or other thorny shrub, be sure to wear thick gloves. First use the pruning shears to cut back the long shoots. This will allow you to start shaping the bush.

2 Cut out any old or diseased wood as close to the main stem as possible.

3 The finished shrub should remain in a good shape with strong, healthy stems bearing flowering shoots.

After use, wipe the blades to get rid of any sap that has accumulated and allow them to dry before closing them. Wipe them regularly with an oiled cloth, and keep the pivoting bolt oiled so that it moves freely and does not strain the wrist. If the pruning shears have a spring, oil it twice a year to repel rust and keep it moving easily.

The blades will need sharpening with an oil stone at least once a season and more often if they are used intensively. In the event of serious damage, many manufacturers sell replacement blades, and some even have a servicing department that can overhaul your pruning shears if necessary.

LOPPERS
These tools resemble long-handled pruning shears and have a similar bypass or anvil blade arrangement. Loppers are used to cut through woody stems that would be too thick for traditional pruning shears, and are ideal for removing old stems on vigorous shrubs like philadelphus or for cutting old rose stumps that can build up at the base of bushes. The long handles give you good leverage on thicker stems and will reach into or up to branches you could not otherwise cut. Make sure there are shock-absorbing stoppers.

LONG-ARM PRUNERS
These are used for pruning tree branches that would normally be out of reach, and can cut through branches up to one inch thick. They consist of a pole 6–9 feet in length, with a hooked anvil and curved blade at the tip, the blade operated by a lever at the opposite end.

Some models are available with an interchangeable pruning saw or a small basket attachment that fits close to the blade for picking fruit without the need to use a ladder. However, doing this from below means you must take care not to remove next year's fruit buds at harvest time.

SMALL CUTTING TOOLS
Floral scissors are used for the very lightest of cutting around the garden, shaping houseplants, and for flower arranging. They have large handgrips in relation to the size of the blades and thin, finely-pointed blades for accuracy. (For more information on cutting fresh flowers, see pages 88–89.)

Powerful cutting
The long handles on loppers give you greater leverage than pruning shears, allowing you to cut larger branches.

Garden snips look like a cross between scissors and bypass pruning shears, but they have much narrower blades than pruning shears and are used for tasks such as thinning and harvesting grapes.

KNIVES
Gardening knives come in dozens of shapes and sizes, each suited to a different purpose. Whichever model you choose should be well-balanced, strong, light, and comfortable to use, with a sharp cutting edge.

General-purpose knives are ideal for the rough jobs in the garden, such as cutting string and opening bags of compost or fertilizer. They may have just one blade, or a multitude of accessories in the one unit.

Care should always be taken when handling a knife, particularly when closing it, so that it does not snap shut on your fingers. Clean the blade thoroughly after use to get rid of any sap. Wipe it with an oiled rag occasionally to keep it rust-free (removing any remaining oil before using it again). A knife in regular use will need sharpening every few weeks, and it is worth getting a fine sharpening stone to keep the

THE MAKING OF KNIVES

Like good-quality cutlery, a garden knife should be comfortable to hold and feel satisfyingly heavy in your hand. It should have a razor-sharp blade that makes the cleanest of cuts and, if it folds up, should open and close easily, even with wet hands. The best folding knives have a locking mechanism to prevent the blade from closing while you are using it.

Many factory-made knives are first-rate, but the crème de la crème are the hand-crafted models. These can be expensive, but they will last you a life-time. Particularly interesting are knives that marry traditional manufacturing techniques with a modern design or materials.

Handmade pocket knives

The basic shapes for the handle and blade are laser-cut from sheets of steel, and then shaped, sharpened, and polished by hand.

1 FOLDING THE HANDLE Made from one piece of metal, the handle is folded in half to create a receptacle for the blade.

2 TIGHTENING THE HANDLE Once folded, the metal is placed in a vice to create a space into which the blade can fit.

3 CREATING THE BLADES The flat pieces of metal for the blades are ground down to a fine point.

4 ASSEMBLING THE COMPONENTS After the metal has been treated with heat and liquid nitrogen to harden the steel, the blades and handles are fixed together, and the finishing process and polishing begins.

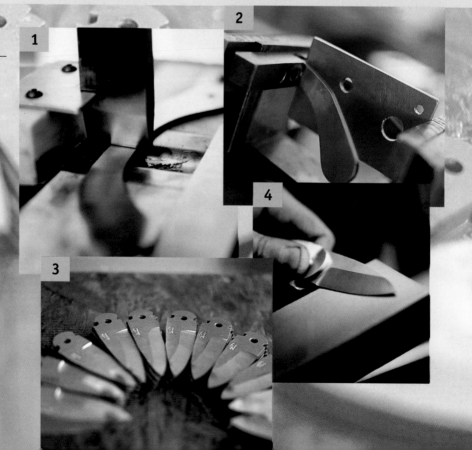

A clean cut

You will need a knife with a straight blade (left) for working on your potting bench. A cutting knife (center) allows you to remove a stem with minimal damage to the parent plant. A curved blade (right) is helpful for slicing into rootstocks.

blade in the best condition. Too coarse a stone will wear the blade away very quickly. (See pages 148–149 for advice on sharpening knives.)

Pruning knives You can identify a pruning knife by its weight, its bulky, often curved handle, and its concave blade. The curve of the blade helps when cutting through thicker shoots. Some also have a mini-saw that folds into the handle.

Budding knives Blunt-ended, these are used when propagating plants, such as roses, by transferring the bud from a selected variety to a rootstock. They are light and thin-bladed because of the delicate nature of the work they do, slicing thin segments of plant tissue without causing excessive damage. They also tend to have a curved knob or "bark lifter" at the end of the blade that, if you twist the knife after making a cut in the stock, will hold open the cut while you insert the bud with the other hand.

Grafting and cuttings knives Both grafting and cuttings knives have similar straight blades, but the handle of the grafting knife is usually curved, whereas that of the cuttings knife is slimmer and straight. The grafting knife is used for propagating plants, such as conifers, by transferring a piece of the selected variety to a rootstock. The cuttings knife is used for taking all types of cuttings (short pieces of shoot that can form roots and grow) from selected plants.

HEDGE TOOLS

Once your hedge has reached its optimum height, you will have to trim it to keep it vigorous and healthy. Your choice of a hand-operated, electric, or fuel-powered hedge trimmer will usually be governed by how much hedge you have to cut and how often it needs trimming. For a short or slow-growing hedge, like yew or box, that needs cutting only a few times each season, hand shears will probably suffice. For a long or fast-growing coniferous hedge, you may need the help of a power tool to speed things up.

Cutting your hedge regularly will keep the growth young and bushy, ensuring that the hedge looks attractive and the shoots you are trimming are not too tough and woody for the equipment. Always cut from the base of the hedge upward, so that the cut material can fall freely to the ground, rather than interfering with the work.

SHEARS

Hand-operated hedge shears come in several designs, but they should be strong, light, and comfortable to use, with a sharp cutting edge. Most have straight, carbon steel blades with a deep notch at the base of the blade for cutting thicker stems. Some may even have a nonstick coating for easier cutting and cleaning.

When buying hedge shears, look for comfortable grips that are molded to fit your hands, a blade-length to suit your needs (from 6 to 8 inches), an adjustable tension nut, and shock-absorbers to prevent jarring and injury to your wrists.

To reach across a wide hedge, it is possible to get telescopic shears with handles that extend from 13 to 20 inches and lock into position. The handles may be made of wood, polypropylene, or aluminum, and the weight will vary accordingly. Choose the pair that fits you and remember, you may be using them for some time if you have to do a lot of cutting, and they will get heavier as your arms get tired.

Single-handed shears Although they will only deal with small, soft shoots, single-handed hedge shears are useful for neatening the hedge between regular cuttings. They are sold by some manufacturers as grass-cutting shears, and have a squeeze grip and two scissor-like blades. The blades swivel around 90 degrees so you can cut a horizontal or vertical plane.

HEDGE TRIMMERS
These are a quick, mechanical means of cutting a hedge and are ideal for gardeners with large expanses of vigorous hedging. Hedge trimmers have two blades,

one on top of the other, each with teeth so that as one blade is drawn backward and forward, the shoots are trapped between the teeth and cut. They may be powered by electricity, battery, or gas. The weight will vary according to the power source and the length of the cutting blade, so select one you can use at any angle on the hedge and with which you will feel comfortable for a prolonged period.

If your hedge is near the power point, choose an electric model that is light, easy, and convenient. However, dragging the cord behind you over a long distance is more difficult and should not be undertaken in wet conditions. It is also essential to keep the cord well away from the working area so there is no danger of cutting through it.

Battery-powered cordless trimmers are light, easy to use, and have a detachable, rechargeable power supply. How long this will last as you cut depends on what you are cutting. More power is needed to cut older, thicker branches and dense wood such as yew, beech, and hornbeam. Thinner, regularly-pruned wood, such as forsythia and privet, is easier to cut through, and the power reserve will last longer.

Gas-driven hedge trimmers have a motor in the handle, and are consequently heavier to operate. The

Pruning hedging conifers
Large vertical plants can be difficult to trim: The head of this gas-powered trimmer swivels so that you can use it at any angle.

Cut down to size

A garden saw (opposite page) is a sturdy implement for pruning most trees. Thick branches and logs are best tackled with a bow saw (far left). Many pruning saws (left) fold away into the handle after use for safe transit and storage.

blade may be interchangeable with a trimmer attachment for cutting rough grass and brambles. This type of trimmer is suitable if you are operating at a great distance from a power source and cutting tough, woody hedges. Rather than purchase a heavy-duty piece of equipment like this, it may be a better idea to rent it for the few times you are likely to need it during the season.

SAWS AND LARGE CUTTING TOOLS

Saws have a multitude of uses in a larger garden, especially if you have trees. The larger ones can be used for cutting up whole trees or branches that blow down in the wind, and removing diseased limbs or those growing outside their allotted space. The smaller saws can be used on woody shrubs and small trees to thin congested growth and remove damaged shoots. Choose the right type of blade for the job at hand: A short blade with closely spaced teeth is best for dealing with smaller branches, a long-bladed saw with less densely spaced teeth for really thick branches.

When buying a new saw, look for a narrow, rounded nose that allows you to work in a tight corner without damaging other branches and has tough, tempered steel blades. Try the grip—with a knuckle protector, in case your hand slips—and make sure it is comfortable. If you choose a folding saw, make sure it has a lock that you can secure in both open and closed positions.

When using a saw, hold the branch beyond the cutting point with your free hand so that it doesn't tear off as the cut deepens, as this would damage the trunk. Pause periodically while you are cutting to clear the teeth of sawdust that will inhibit the cutting action. Clean the blade thoroughly after use, and wipe occasionally with an oiled cloth.

Bow saws These have a curved steel tubing frame and a straight cutting blade with a row of sharp teeth on the outside. The blade is held taut between the arms of the frame and is released by a handle at one end. Use a bow saw for working through larger branches and logs; it will cut on both the forward and backward strokes. They vary in size, shape, and blade length, but the blades are replaceable. For cutting larger branches, they are ideal. Keep a cover over the blade when it is not in use.

Garden saws The general-purpose garden saw is much like a wood saw, in that it is a basic triangular shape with teeth along one edge. It is useful for pruning trees and shrubs, and cutting logs and larger branches where access is difficult for a bow saw. It has small teeth at the tip of the blade to help start off, then larger teeth along the blade for faster cutting. It cuts on both the forward and backward stroke.

Pruning saws Small, hand-held tools with a straight or curved steel blade, pruning saws are useful for cutting larger branches. Several models are available that are particularly suited for use in small spaces and in the narrow angles between branches.

Many are designed to fold, with the blade closing into the handle like a knife for easy storage. These fit neatly into a pocket when not in use and can be carried around easily, but are better used on only moderately thick branches.

Topiary tool kit

The art of shaping and training trees and shrubs has been popular with gardeners for centuries. A lively imagination, some patience, and some sharp cutting implements are the most important tools you'll need.

One of the great things about topiary is that it looks just as at home in a small courtyard or patio as it does in a large, formal garden. A pair of globe-shaped bay trees in containers provide an eye-catching frame for a doorway; a living sculpture makes an arresting impression in front of your home; low box hedges are a good way of creating boundaries for an herb garden, while a small, ivy-covered, wire frame can make a great centerpiece for your dinner table.

Many plants are suitable for topiary. Evergreens are favorites as they provide year-round interest in the garden. For large geometric shapes, bay (*Laurus nobilis*) and holly (*Ilex aquifolium*) are good choices. Box (*Buxus sempervirens*) and slow-growing yew (*Taxus baccata*) are ideal for more complex shapes. Sphagnum moss is good for stuffing wire frames. And creeping fig (*Ficus pumila*) and ivy (*Hedera helix*) are easy to train around wire supports.

Trimming implements

Sharp cutting tools are essential if you are to achieve a nice finish. Large-scale topiary may require electric hedge trimmers to get you started and enable you to establish the basic shape, but trimmers are too crude for the finishing touches.

Good-quality hedge shears are perfect for trimming box hedges in knot gardens and creating geometric shapes. Scissors or pruning shears are better for complicated shapes like animals

Shape up your plants

Growing trailing plants over a wire frame is a quick and easy way of creating a topiary effect (far left and center left). Topiary shears (left) offer maximum control when precision cutting is necessary.

Keep it neat

Cutting in a straight line can be tricky, especially when you are working at an awkward height, so use a length of garden string to help you avoid mistakes.

and spirals. Specialty topiary shears will be very useful if you are a real enthusiast. Held in one hand, these consist of two razor-sharp, carbon-steel blades that are operated by squeezing the double bow shaped handles together. The grip position gives you precise control over the cut, and you can catch the cuttings with your free hand.

Creating a shape

Cones, spirals, and spheres; rabbits, ducks, and other animals; waves, hearts, and abstract designs—you can grow or trim a plant into any shape that inspires you. There are three ways to achieve your aims: You can trim a shrub to the desired shape, which, depending on the design, can require great skill; you can train plants to grow over a wire frame; or you can stuff a frame with moss.

If you are trimming a hedge or shrub into a solid shape, you will probably find it easier to use guides. String and bamboo canes are helpful when you are trying to create a straight line. For curves and more complicated lines, you can use stiff wire.

Frames are available in many different designs from online and traditional brick-and-mortar garden stores. These may be two-dimensional shapes such as hearts and stars, or three-dimensional ones like cones, spirals, and animals. The two-dimensional versions are mainly designed for climbing plants like ivy or creeping fig; simply insert the frame into the ground or container and trail the stems of your plant around the wire as it grows.

For a more solid living sculpture, you'll need to place a three-dimensional frame over a plant

growing in the ground or in a container. As the plant grows, its leaves will start to fill the frame and eventually protrude through the wire—simply trim them back to the shape of the frame.

It isn't difficult to make a simple frame yourself, however; all you need is some sturdy wire and a pair of wire cutters (don't use pruning shears, as the wire will blunt the blades).

Quick topiary

Box, yew, bay, and other traditional topiary plants grow slowly, so you don't have to spend all your precious gardening time trimming and pruning them. The downside is that it can take several years to create a topiary shape. For more immediate results, you can stuff a wire frame with sphagnum moss and then plant, a bit like a hanging basket, fast-growing vine plants. Eventually these plants will spread over the frame, completely hiding the moss. You'll need chicken wire or plastic mesh to cover the frame, clear fishing line to hold the moss in place, and a good pair of gloves, as sphagnum moss can contain bacteria that may cause infection if it comes into contact with an cut. Old bobby pins are useful for holding the new growth in place.

Using a scythe

A scythe (far left) will cope with those dense patches of grassland that might break the cord on a trimmer. A scythette (left) can be used with one hand.

English pruning saws These have a tapering blade with teeth on both sides, one set producing a smoother finished cut than the other. Take care while sawing not to damage nearby branches with the set of teeth not in use.

Grecian saws These have a curved blade tapered to a sharp point and sloping teeth designed to cut on the return stroke. The teeth are large and coarse, enabling them to cut through soft, wet, live wood.

Straight-bladed saws The shape of the teeth varies according to whether it is designed to cut on just the pull stroke or on both the push and pull.

CHAINSAWS

These are heavy-duty cutting tools, used for felling trees and cutting up larger logs. They may be powered by electricity or gas, and operate as the motor sends a toothed, cutting chain traveling around the perimeter of a long, oval, metal guide bar. The gas-driven types are heavier than electric ones, and they come in a range of sizes according to their intended use. Choose one that feels balanced in your hands and has a good guard over the grip to protect your hand. Unless you have a lot of woodland, you are unlikely to need a chain saw very often, and it will probably be as easy to

rent one for a day. Safety is paramount when operating a chain saw (see page 129) as it is sharp, fast-moving and heavy, and if there is a knot in the wood you are cutting, the bar will kick back out. You will need gloves, goggles, ear protection, steel-toed boots, and a helmet as basic essentials. Snag-proof trousers are a bonus. Long hair must be tied out of the way, and you should take off, or fasten, any loose clothing.

SCYTHE

This is a very sharp, curved, carbon-steel blade mounted on a long wood or tubular steel shaft (the snath), with a wooden handgrip at the top and another adjustable one mounted partway down to

Cutting and clearing tools

A well-stocked shed would include a scythe, a rake, and a hay fork (the long-handled tools at the front); a sickle leans against the wall on the lower right.

Go for the chop

Use an ax (far left) to chop larger logs, and a hatchet (left) to cut up kindling and small branches.

make it easier to use. It is useful for cutting through long or rough grass, and the heavier models can also cut through bramble stems and scrub. It was the traditional implement used for harvesting corn, and an accomplished user can quickly cut through a large area with a rhythmic swinging motion—and a very sharp blade. The length of the swing needed to wield this properly means that it is not easy to stop if you spot an obstruction, so it is best used on areas you know to be without large stones. Clean, sharpen, and wipe the blade with an oiled cloth after each use to keep the effort needed to use it to a minimum.

SICKLES

These have a very sharp curved blade mounted on a short wooden or plastic handle. You should use them low to the ground for trimming rough grass where rocks may be hidden. They need to be kept very sharp to work well. Most are made for right-handed users and may be difficult for left-handed gardeners to wield.

BILLHOOKS

Traditionally used for maintenance of hedges and hedge laying, billhooks have a sharp, curved blade—like a bird's beak—often with a flat-edged blade on the back. They can be mounted on a short handle for closer work (with rivets or a tang-and-ferrule joint) or a longer hickory shaft (with rivets). Those with long shafts are ideal for hacking through tough undergrowth.

Similar implements are available, known as slashers or brush hooks. These also have a long shaft and a curved blade for cutting through brush and thickets. Reap and grass hooks are hand-held, with a long, curved blade for cutting through rough grass and overgrown weeds.

AXES AND HATCHETS

The ax is not a subtle implement, but it is unrivaled for splitting logs and chopping out old tree stumps. It consists of a delta-shaped, carbon-steel head, tempered and hardened for durability, fitted onto a wooden handle. The wood used is often hickory, chosen for its strength, and should be smooth and splinter-free. The head should also be smooth, with no obvious blemishes where it could crack under strain. Use all sizes of ax in a swinging motion, with both hands. The hatchet is essentially a smaller version of the ax, with a shorter handle that you can use with one hand.

SHREDDERS

Garden shredders are designed to make light work of chopping prunings, fallen leaves, and other debris into a manageable mulch. It is important to consider the size of your garden and how much waste it will generate before you buy a shredder. If you only shred once or twice a year, you may as well rent one for the day rather than have it sitting in the shed. However, if you make your own compost and are likely to shred everything you prune throughout the year, it will be a good investment. (See page 101 for more on shredders.)

5

Planting
and Sowing

The potting bench

Planting and sowing are two of the most exciting aspects of gardening because they represent new beginnings and the promise of things to come. It's hard to beat the thrilling sense of achievement you feel when the first tiny shoots start to appear on the first plants you grow from seed. As they get larger, your next target is to keep them healthy as you move them outside or into larger pots. Plants that you buy when young and vulnerable require similar care and provide similar exciting rewards.

PLANTING TOOLS

The tools for the first stage in a plant's life are necessarily small to deal with the detailed handling involved. Using too large an implement could prove fatal to a delicate little plant. You should also prepare the soil to a fine tilth for the seedlings to survive—even if you are sowing seed directly into a seedbed outdoors (as with vegetables, for instance). If you try to sow seed where the soil lumps are large, there will be too many air pockets, and a tiny root will wither

before it reaches its target of soil. Marking out the rows before you start will allow you to track where you have sown the seed, and clear markers will remind you what it was.

MEASURING RODS

If you are marking out several rows for seeds or planting a hedge with the plants at set spacings, then one of the easiest ways of keeping the distance consistent is to use a measuring rod. This is a piece of wood, about 6 feet long, marked at 3–6 inch intervals. Lay it on the ground next to where you are working, and use the marks to determine your spacings. For

Growing your own

If you have the space, dedicate an area of your garden shed to potting (right). Here you can store unused containers and work comfortably at a potting bench. Young plants are difficult to tell apart, so make sure you label them (above).

Soil scoop

This tool has a sharp point that enables you to dig small holes, and serrated edges to cut through root bound soil. The curved tip prevents soil from slipping off.

close spacings, use every mark, but for wider gaps, use alternate marks or one in three. You can make your own measuring rod by calibrating a long piece of wood or straight bamboo cane.

GARDEN LINE

To allow you to work along a straight line between two points you will need a garden line. This strong twine or polypropylene thread is brightly colored—

usually orange—making it easy to spot and avoid when it is lying against the soil. Wind it around two metal or plastic spools, each with a spike to drive it firmly into the soil. Make a loop with the twine to fit over the spike before pushing it into the ground, to keep surplus twine from distorting the line you are trying to keep.

A garden line is useful for marking out a drill for sowing seed in the vegetable garden, although you can just as easily use it to mark the edge of a lawn you are laying or recutting. Sow the seed in the drill, cover it lightly with soil, and simply lift the line to move to the next position.

LABELS

With all the work involved in planting or sowing, it is easy to overlook the task of labeling the plants—the most obvious method of recording what has been sown or planted, and when. If they are beyond the seedling stage, with obvious markings, flower colors, or leaf shapes, then you should find it easy to distinguish one from another. Where you are sowing seed, however, this is much more difficult, as seedlings often have very similar seed leaves, especially within the same plant family (as with vegetables).

When you have regular crops, you can use plastic labels season after season. Clean them between crops if you change variety, or write them in permanent marker for use with the same one. Where you are planting more permanently with shrubs, climbers, and trees in the garden, you can use an ornamental label—such as metal or plastic tape—with the letters embossed on it.

TROWEL

Hand trowels have a multitude of uses within the garden, their size making them suitable for many detailed tasks. (See page 36 for more information.) The width of the trowel head varies slightly according to whether it is designed for general garden tasks, or for thinning out and replanting seedlings and small plants. Use it like a small spade for pushing under the plant and lifting it out of the soil, or for digging a small planting hole.

Planting out

A measuring rod (left) is invaluable when planting at even distances is important. Use a garden line (center) to sow in a straight line. Labels come in a huge range of shapes and sizes (right).

If the blade of the trowel has depth markings on it, it is intended primarily for planting bulbs. The markings are a quick and easy guide to how deep you are pushing the trowel into the soil, as you plant each bulb at its appropriate depth. Too deep, and the bulb may not live long enough for the shoot to reach the surface. Too shallow and it may push itself out of the soil as the roots develop, or you may damage it as you

Specialist trowels

A calibrated trowel (far left) is especially helpful when the depth of planting is critical, for example when transplanting or planting bulbs. A right-angled trowel (left) is ideal for transferring seedlings into the ground: Simply pull the blade toward you to open a hole in the soil and then pop in the plant.

Bulb planters

These can be short-handled (below) or long-handled (right). The latter often have a T-bar at the base to press down on with your foot.

cultivate nearby soil. A bulb-planting trowel is also useful for transplanting, where you need to set all young plants at the same depth.

You can find trowels made entirely of polypropylene, or with heads of carbon steel, stainless steel, or aluminum with a tang-and-ferrule joint into a wooden handle. Carbon-steel models may have a nonstick coating to reduce the chance of corrosion or soil sticking to them (making them heavier to use). Some have ergonomic handles to ease strain on the wrists.

HAND FORK

Like the hand trowel, the diminutive size of the hand fork means that it is suited to close, detailed work. Use one hand fork to prepare a small area of soil for planting—such as a seedbed between established plants—or use two forks back-to-back to divide an established plant. You can split a congested clump of iris into several smaller clumps and replant them further apart by pushing both forks into the large clump, together but back-to-back, and then pry them apart to divide the matted growth. Repeat this until the new clumps are the required size. Give any surplus away to friends—trading for new varieties—or compost them.

Forks may be made of polypropylene throughout, or with a head of carbon steel, stainless steel, or aluminum with a wooden handle. As with trowels, carbon-steel models often have a nonstick coating.

BULB PLANTERS

The easiest way to plant a number of bulbs for a massed effect is to consign them to a trench or hole. However, if you are planting bulbs individually, then a bulb planter is a useful tool. It has a cylindrical "blade," so that when it is pushed into the soil, it removes a circular core. Place the bulb at the bottom of the hole, and then crumble the soil removed from the hole back over the bulb and firm it gently. If you are planting into grass, the process is the same, with the circle of turf replaced on top of the crumbled soil.

You can find bulb planters with short, D-shaped, wooden or plastic handles for close use, or with long, T-shaped handles designed for use while standing. Some have hinged blades that open to allow the plug of soil to fall free of the blades more easily.

DIBBERS

The dibber dates far back in gardening history and was originally made from the handle of a broken wooden spade or fork, sharpened to a blunt point. It was ideal for making a small planting hole for transplanting seedlings. Today's dibber may be a straight bar of wood (with or without ornamental turnings) or have a T-, L- or D-shaped handle. The tip

Dibbers and widgers

If you grow a lot of plants from seed, you'll want a dibber or two in your tool kit. Use a narrow dibber (left), also known as a widger, for small seeds and seedlings, and a wider tool (far left) for larger ones or small bulbs.

may be metal to protect the wood from wear and tear. Dibbers are ideal for planting seedlings or plug plants into the garden. For "pricking out" seedlings, where a finer point is required, slim, plastic dibbers are useful, and these often have points at both ends, one smaller than the other.

SIEVES

When you are sowing fine seed, you need the finest possible tilth of soil above and below the seed, so that the seedlings are not overwhelmed. A garden sieve (or "riddle") will easily allow you to prepare a fine tilth. Once the seed is sown, use the sieve to cover the seedbed with fine particles of soil. It can also be used for sieving topsoil or compost over the lawn to top-dress it. Shake out any stones, twigs, or small plants trapped in the mesh, and dispose of these elsewhere.

Sieves have a circular frame of wood, plastic, or steel, with the mesh stretched over one side. The mesh varies in hole size, according to the size of particles you want to create. Some models are equipped with interchangeable screens. In order to be fully effective, the soil needs to be moist enough to break up easily. A large quantity can be placed in and pushed through the sieve, as it is shaken over the area to be covered and does not all land in one place.

Sowing seed

1 Fill a seed tray with seed compost. Remove any surplus, then tamp it down very gently. Don't press too firmly, or the roots will find it hard to penetrate. Moisten the surface of the soil.

2 Sprinkle the seeds evenly over the soil. If the seeds are very fine, you may need to mix them with dry sand so you can see how much you have sown.

3 Cover the seeds with sieved soil, according to the instructions on the packet, and position the tray so that it receives plenty of light (but not direct sunlight).

4 After germination has occurred, and one or two true leaves have developed, the plants are ready for transferring to another container.

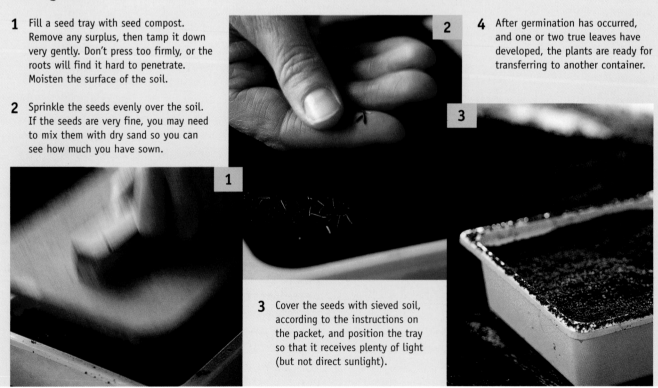

For good tilth

Give your seedlings the best chance of survival by using a sieve to aerate and take the lumps out of soil.

PROPAGATING TOOLS

The seeds of many plants are too fragile to sow directly into the ground, so you will need to start them indoors.

SEED TRAYS

Get a head start in spring by using seed trays, also known as flats, to grow plants indoors. You can sow them while the weather is still too cold to plant outdoors, and keep them in the protected conditions of the house, greenhouse, or cold frame until conditions outside improve. Once they are big enough, you can transplant or "prick out" the seedlings into separate pots prior to planting outside.

Seed trays are usually plastic and rectangular in shape, and come in full and half sizes according to the quantity of seed you are sowing. They are reusable once they have been washed clean, and should have drainage holes in the base to prevent waterlogging.

MODULES

These are predivided seed trays that allow you to sow the seed and transplant it some time later without disturbing its roots. When the young plant is ready to transplant, it and its roots can be moved as a block without the need to dig it up. This reduces the chance of it suffering a transplanting shock that can impede growth for weeks.

The number of modules per tray varies and can reach up to about eighty. They are ideal for growing larger seed (such as string beans), which can be sown at one or two seeds to each module, or very fine seed (such as lobelia) where a pinch of seeds are sown together, germinate together, and will produce a small clump of plants ideal for bedding or display in a hanging basket. You can wash and reuse some plastic trays; others are broken into sections as the plants are

Flowers by design

There are few more welcoming sights than a carefully-crafted cut-flower display. Composed in a complementary vase, they make fascinating talking points. But aside from their beauty, there are other reasons for bringing flowers indoors.

Away from the garden where pests, wind, rain, and hail can damage opening blooms, buds unfold pristinely and perfectly. Bringing flowers indoors also lets us study their intricate and sensuous shapes. Outdoors, their transient beauty often passes unseen. In a vase, flowers can be admired for days—weeks even.

Arranging flowers is a challenge to your creative skills. If you're new to the art form, initial efforts can be a muddle of heights and colors, but as experience grows, you will learn how to associate shapes, textures, and colors. You will also discover that certain tools and accessories help to achieve good results.

Cutting tools

First of all, choose a good pair of pruning shears that not only slice through stems but grip them too—a big benefit when gathering thorny roses. You will also need them for recutting "tired" ends of woody shoots to expose fresh, water-conducting vessels.

Use a craft knife with a fixed, open blade to cut stem ends—slicing obliquely or splitting—to help them absorb water. Also use it to remove thorns and leaves.

Short bladed floral scissors—with one serrated blade—are invaluable for cutting stems without crushing them, whereas normal household scissors can damage tissues. There should be ample handle space for fingers and thumb. Most also have a notch for cutting thin wire.

You will need some wire cutters to hand if you are using chicken wire (as a prop for tall, heavy stems) or thick wire (for supporting dried flowers or for binding blooms so that they form a posy or corsage).

Keeping flowers fresh

A bucket is essential for plunging flowers up to their necks immediately after cutting them. This ensures that the stems are fully charged with moisture. Choose a type with two side handles, rather than one swinging handle, which may damage your blooms if the handle is not positioned carefully.

Gathering the harvest

Cut right through the stalk of your flower at an oblique angle (far left) to increase the area that will be exposed to water. Use pruning shears (center left) on tough and woody stems, and a budding knife (left) to avoid damaging any of the bark.

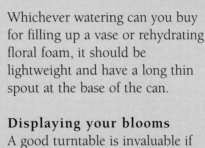

Attractive arrangements

To give a display lasting form and structure, wind thin wire around the head and stems of the tallest flowers (center). Colored ribbon is ideal for tying bouquets and posies (above). But watch you don't blunt your garden scissors cutting the ribbon—use fabric scissors (bottom) instead.

Whichever watering can you buy for filling up a vase or rehydrating floral foam, it should be lightweight and have a long thin spout at the base of the can.

Displaying your blooms

A good turntable is invaluable if you are creating a display to be viewed from all sides. It will save you from constantly lifting the vase to check the height, angle, and balance of your flowers and foliage.

Few flower arrangers can do without a little floral foam, soaked and used in a vase to support cut flower stems. Once you have cut it to shape, place this cellular material in the vase or other container. Insert stems into it to hold them firmly at any angle. There are two types of foam: green, which is used in water, and brown or gray.

After green foam is soaked in water, it absorbs up to thirty times its weight, enabling flowers arranged in it to stay fresher for longer than in water alone. Once wet, green floral foam must not dry out. If you want to use it for several arrangements, wrap it in foil between uses. Large displays may need support from chicken wire. Flowers with mucilaginous sap, such as anemones, daffodils, and tulips, should not be arranged in foam for they have difficulty absorbing water from it and are better displayed in a pin-holder (see below).

The other form of floral foam is brown or gray and should be kept dry. Use it to support arrangements of dried or artificial flowers.

Also known as "kenzan" (a Japanese term), the pin-holder is another favorite of flower arrangers. It has a multitude of sharply pointed, circular, or rectangular pins that rise from a heavy, ideally brass, base allowing you to insert flower stems between them, ensuring an even, balanced display. Use adhesive clay to stick the pin-holder to the base of a vase or bowl. However, a container isn't necessary if you choose a pin-holder that his its own water reservoir in the base. Ask for one like this when buying if you'd find it more useful.

WHICH POT IS BEST FOR YOU?

There's no need to take a seedling out of its peat pot when you prick it out, which means less chance of transplant shock; peat pots can't be reused, however, so are not the best value option.

Plastic pots are light, durable, reusable, and retain moisture well; they can encourage unhealthy patterns of root growth, though, which may contribute to transplant shock.

Small metal containers are not cheap but they are attractive and contemporary, making them a good choice if you don't want to transplant the plants.

airtight package, and should be treated as any other pot up to the point of planting. Fill each to the brim with compost, insert the plant, and water. The peat will soak up water as well as the compost, and a close check should be kept to ensure that they are always moist, as moisture evaporates from the sides as well as the top.

Roots will usually start to appear through the sides and base of the pot before the plant is put into its final container, indicating that the plant is ready to move on. To replant the seedling, make a hole in the ground or in compost in a new container large enough to accommodate the peat pot, and treat the pot as a rootball, covering it over with the new compost.

Plastic pots While diminutive plastic pots may be unsuitable for use in the garden, being unstable in the wind, they make very practical containers for young plants indoors. Durable and recyclable, they don't lose water as quickly as peat pots, but you will need to transplant the plants once they grow too big.

PROPAGATORS

Sometimes seeds and cuttings need a little extra protection to become established and form a good root system. Some plants are particularly fussy, and won't grow unless the compost reaches a certain temperature and humidity. In order to meet such

removed; some trays are thin and will serve you for one season only. Modules made of peat have the added advantage of being degradable, so there is no need to take the plant out of the tray. Simply divide the tray into separate parts and plant the whole module. The roots will grow out through the sides of the module into the soil or compost.

POTS FOR SEEDLINGS AND YOUNG PLANTS

Small containers for small plants come in a variety of materials, including terra cotta, metal and the two favorites: peat and plastic. Regardless of the type you choose, always use clean pots and fresh compost.

Peat pots Made of dried, compressed peat, these small containers degrade once they are in the soil or compost, so there is no need to remove the plant from within it as it is planted out. This means less root disturbance, which can halt growth until the plant recovers. They are supplied packed together in an

Lantern cloches

Square and octagonal lantern cloches can be useful alternatives to the bell shape. The lift-off lids make for easy ventilation.

requirements, you may need to buy a special case known as a propagator. These vary from a simple plastic tray with a clear plastic cover designed to keep the air temperature and humidity levels high, to more complex cases with heating cables in the base that warm the compost (rooting zone) as well. The larger cases have a layer of sand in the base over the warming cables so that there is a residual level of heat, maintaining a constant temperature.

The plastic cover should be sturdy and clear to allow as much light through as possible (although you may need to shade the plants if they are growing in bright sunlight). Look for one with a vent you can open to raise and lower the levels of heat and humidity inside, as this will give you much greater control. Wash the cover regularly to prevent algae or fungus from thriving in the moist, warm conditions.

CLOCHES AND COLD FRAMES

Young plants are vulnerable to the cold, particularly if they have been started off indoors. The answer is to use a cloche or cold frame, which shelters plants from the elements. The added warmth and protection from wind, frost, birds, and insects will enable you to plant tomatoes, lettuce, and other young plants a couple of weeks earlier in the season than you could in open ground; ripen crops such as strawberries more

Propagators

Create a suitable environment for seedlings with an electric propagator (far left), which allows you to set the desired temperature; simpler versions consist of a seed tray with a ventilated clear plastic cover (left.)

speedily; and extend the growing season. A cloche is a dome-shaped cover, named after the French word for "bell," designed to warm the soil for early planting or to protect the plants underneath from the weather. Victorian cloches were like miniature greenhouses, with glazed panels, or bell-shaped glass domes; some could be ventilated, others had to be removed to allow air to circulate. These types of glass cloches are still available today, but plastic varieties are just as effective. Mini versions are excellent for seedlings. Alternatively, you can use plastic sheeting to form a low tunnel over wire hoops, with the ends and sides buried into the soil.

Larger than cloches, cold frames are traditionally wooden-framed structures with glass roofs that keep the light and warmth in. Versions are also available in lighter-weight materials. The roof is usually hinged, so you can increase the ventilation when necessary.

SUPPORTING YOUR PLANTS

Plants need to be staked to prevent them being damaged by wind, either directly (as the wind causes the shoots to hit each other or a solid object) or indirectly (when the movement of the plant in the soil loosens the rootball, breaks the roots, and makes the plant unstable).

Keep small or thin plants in place using bamboo canes of various lengths and thicknesses. Push the cane into the soil next to the plant and secure the stem to it using twine, raffia, or a plastic tie. It is important to check these ties regularly or they may

Keeping upright

Bamboo canes, wooden pea sticks, and slim plastic stakes make great props for seedlings and small plants. Larger shrubs, trees, and climbers will need sturdier supports, such as metal or wooden stakes.

- You have a balcony, terrace, window box, patio, deck, steps, or roof garden that would benefit from a splash of color.
- You like the flexibility offered by container gardening.

Don't forget that plants in pots require a bit more TLC than those growing in the ground: They need regular watering and feeding, especially in the growing season.

CHOOSING CONTAINERS

Pots come in an enormous variety of prices, sizes, and materials, ranging from the traditional terra-cotta and stone, to plastic, reconstituted stone, concrete, wood, metal, rubber, and fiberglass.

Be sure to match the size of the container to the size of the plant. The rootball should fit comfortably into the pot, with some space to expand. Large containers retain moisture more efficiently, an important point to consider as soil in pots tends to dry out much more quickly than it does in the ground. On the other hand, large containers are difficult to maneuver, especially once they have been filled.

Weight is another consideration, particularly if your garden is on a balcony or roof. Pots become much heavier when they are watered, so check that the structure of your roof or balcony can support the extra weight.

Your choice of shape and style will be a matter of taste. Broadly speaking, traditional urns and decorative pots will suit a formal garden; simple styles will complement a more modern design. Think, too, about the type of plants you wish to place in the container. If they are likely to trail over the sides of the pot, hiding most of it from view, then it hardly matters what the pot is made of, but if you are growing a slow-growing subject, such as a cactus, you may wish to choose a more attractive container. You could always customize old containers—for instance, a plain metal bucket can be transformed with a verdigris paint finish.

begin to cut into the stem as it expands. If this happens, the stem will break at that point the next time it is put under any stress. Canes can be used to guide climbing plants to their permanent growing frame and support lighter plants and flowers.

Larger plants and trees will need a more substantial wooden stake to help them establish after planting. At this time, they are particularly susceptible to the wind until the roots have anchored into the soil. A short stake, driven into the soil next to the rootball and tied to the tree at the base, will keep the roots still enough to anchor while allowing the trunk to flex and thicken as it should. By the time the wooden stake rots, the tree should be able to withstand high winds.

Trellises provide a surface for climbing plants to cling to and can be used to divide areas of the garden. Plastic trellises are available, but wooden versions tend to be more popular; both come in a variety of colors.

Other supports for your plants include wigwams, obelisks, arches, and pergolas. These may be of bamboo, willow, hardwood, pressure-treated softwood, and metal.

POTS AND CONTAINERS

There are many reasons why you might want some plants to live permanently in a container rather than in the ground:

- The soil in your garden is unsuitable for certain species; containers are the perfect solution, as you can fill these with compost specially suited to particular plants.
- You prefer to have plants such as herbs close to the kitchen.

Container gardening

Choose pots with a wide base that are stable in the wind. Narrow-necked urns may look fabulous, but you'll find it difficult to repot the plants within. Frostproof containers are vital if you live in an area with cold winters.

Plastic pots can be washed and reused, and don't need quite so much watering. They are available in a wide range of sizes, from tiny to huge, and are relatively inexpensive. They are ideal for outdoor plants as the intermediate and temporary stage between the seed tray and the final position. But they are more likely to topple over in the wind than their terra-cotta cousins, and can become brittle when in direct sunlight.

Wood makes a lovely material for containers, but check that the pot is made from hardwood or pressure-treated softwood: otherwise it is liable to rot.

Stone is frostproof and very attractive, but tends to be expensive, so reconstituted stone is a more affordable option. Both can be very heavy.

Metal, and especially galvanized steel, is a popular choice in the contemporary garden. But bear in mind that metal is an efficient conductor of heat, so the soil inside can be poorly insulated. Fiberglass containers are available in a variety of colors, and are durable and lightweight.

Terra-cotta pots look pleasing, are porous (meaning excess moisture can drain away), and allow air to circulate around the roots of the plant. On the other hand, they are easily broken and lose a considerable amount of moisture through their sides, requiring more watering. Some are also susceptible to frost damage.

SOIL TESTING

The type of soil in your garden will affect how well particular plants will grow. For example, some plants, such as rhododendrons, camellias, and heathers, thrive in acid conditions, whereas others, including dianthus and thyme, do better in alkaline soils. To find out the pH (or level of acidity/alkalinity) of your soil, you will need a soil testing kit.

Testing kits are inexpensive and available at most garden stores. To test one area, take a sample from about 6 inches down into the soil, and use a funnel or piece of paper to pour the soil into the testing bottle. Add water following the manufacturer's instructions, shake, and check the results against the color chart supplied. A pH level of 6.5–7 is regarded as neutral; below neutral is acid, above it is alkaline. To test the whole garden, you can get a representative sample by taking 5 or 6 small amounts from the same depth around the garden and mixing them together. If you find that your soil is unsuited to a favorite plant of yours, you can grow it in a container instead, filled with the appropriate type of compost.

6

Tidying the Garden

A clean sweep

The more efficiently you tidy up your garden, the more time you will have to enjoy it. And that's what gardening is: a blend of satisfaction and happy exercise that comes from growing plants to the best of your ability. Many tools have been developed to assist cleaning—from brushes for paths and drives, electric leaf collectors and blowers, and time-saving devices to hasten your efforts when breaking down prunings.

BROOMS

These are necessary for keeping the hard surfaces of the garden tidy. There are two main types: besoms and push brooms. The besom is a bundle of twigs wired to a handle and used with a sideways sweeping action. The more popular push broom has a head of bristles with a texture ranging from soft to extra stiff. Handles are replaceable whether they are hardwood (usually ash), heavy-duty plastic, or aluminum. The broom is named after a small, wild shrub (of the same name) with butterfly-shaped, yellow pea flowers.

BESOM BROOMS

These are among the oldest tools conceived by humans. Our cave-dwelling ancestors used bunches of twiggy branches to tidy up their living quarters. Today

Time to brush up

The besom brush is ideal for clearing fall leaves and other debris from your lawn.

they are made by tightly fixing birch or heather twigs with a wire and metal strap to a stocky pole. They are used for sweeping leaves and bulky litter from paths and patios, or gently teasing fallen twigs and leaves from among border plants. A well-made besom, with plenty of brush like a fox's tail, is a pleasure to use and lasts for years. When not in use, it's best stored upside down to keep the head from becoming misshapen.

PUSH BROOMS

There are several versions of the conventional push broom which you stand behind and gently push. Use a soft-bristled head for collecting fine, dusty debris around the house, or in a shed or workshop. Opt for a stiffer, springy-bristled head for collecting twigs and other large debris from a patio, path, drive, or yard. Bristles are made from hardwearing natural fibers, PVC, or polypropylene. If you have a large area to sweep and need a reliable broom that won't let you down, opt for one that has a reinforced handle with a metal brace for extra stability.

Patio brooms These have short and stocky heads, around 10 inches long, with soft, medium, or stiff bristles. Garden brooms are wider and equally versatile. Some brooms have a dual-handle slot allowing you to move the handle from one side of the head to the other when the bristles wear down

The right broom for the job

The bristles of push brooms (above left) come in different densities—the stiffer they are, the larger the debris they will pick up; hand brushes (center) are perfect for sweeping sand into cracks in the lawn; choose an American shaker brush (above right) for sweeping your patio or deck.

unequally. To keep the lawn and patio free from garbage with one tool, use a combined PVC lawn rake and stiff-bristled broom.

Broom handles The warmest handles are made from wood or plastic-sleeved metal—an important consideration if you are sweeping in winter when bare metal can be exceptionally cold.

Though many brooms come with a wooden handle screwed into the head, some have a useful quick-change system. In this instance, you can replace a broom head with a hoe, rake, or another tool head

"And add to these retired Leisure
That in trim gardens takes his pleasure."
JOHN MILTON, POET (1608–1674)

Lawn and leaf rakes

A mini or hand fan rake (left) has a short handle and is perfect for collecting unwanted material from around particular plants; the small sweep rake (center) has round, flexible tines and a longer handle; expanding varieties (right) enable you to adjust the span of the rake to suit your needs.

(see boxed feature, page 100). Handles are short, medium, or long, but an adjustable, telescopic handle is a good idea if more than one person uses the same broom. Further refinements include a T-shaped handle for precise control of the broom around delicate edging plants.

Prolong the life of your broom by storing it on its handle to avoid distorting bristles, and preserve wooden handles by coating them with linseed oil if they start to look or feel dried out.

FAN RAKES

Fall leaves are likely to scatter attractively in your garden from the first winds of late summer, but ignore them at your peril. Harboring potential pests and diseases, they should be cleared regularly before winter rains turn them into sludge. Collect them from between border plants, from the surface of your lawn, and from under shrubs and hedges for composting into a useful mulch.

The ideal tool for this task is the fan or leaf rake, which differs from the garden rake in that its tines are arranged in a fan shape. Use it much as you would a conventional rake for pulling leaves, twigs, or grass clippings from among plants.

For closely planted beds at ground level or raised beds and borders, it's best to use a flexible model. It can be short- or long-handled, with steel or plastic tines, but it should not be too wide, as flared rakes are liable to damage shoots and buds.

Whichever type you select, use it carefully to avoid damaging tines, because, when misaligned, these can be difficult to repair. Lubricate metal parts regularly to control rust.

SMALL FAN RAKE

A variant of the standard fan rake, the mini version has many virtues. A short, contoured handle ensures a firm grip and reduces slipping, and its nine thin, flat, springy, steel tines are designed to caress the soil and remove debris without harming plants. It's neither too heavy nor too lightweight, and while you work with it you can assess your plants' general health.

SMALL SWEEP RAKE

The comb-like small sweep is a rake you can rely on. Its tines, bent at right angles at the tip, gently remove leaves and other debris from crown buds. To increase its flexibility, use two lengths of handle—a short one for getting in close to plants that need special care, and a longer one for removing litter from the back of a border or from beneath a hedge.

Removing piles of debris

Long-handled metal grabbers (inset) allow you to remove garden refuse without bending down; hand grabbers are just as efficient, but you do need to reach down.

EXPANDING RAKE

This is a voracious rake with a catchment area ranging from 12 to 19 inches. Its 22 tines slot into a semi-circular adjuster which you can slide up or down to expand or contract the fan, depending on the size of the area you are clearing and the type of material you wish to tackle.

GRABBING RAKES

Transferring the piles of raked leaves, grass mowings, hedge trimmings, and other garbage to a cart presents further choices. The easiest method is to grip the debris between two rectangular boards and lift it into the barrow. However, this entails bending, which may be a problem if you have a weak back. A better solution is to buy a purpose-made leaf collector made from galvanized steel. One model looks like a pair of giant sugar tongs with aligned jaws that cleanly pick up the smallest heap of debris. Another type has large, toothed, polypropylene jaws which you open and close around the heap. To maintain, clean the metal-jawed version with a wooden spatula to remove caked mud and spray with lubricant before storing.

One leaf collector looks like a giant pair of baseball gloves. Made from heavy-duty plastic with toothed jaws, it comes with hand-fastening straps. You will, of course, have to bend to use it—but regular bending tones up stomach muscles.

BLOWERS AND VACUUMS

You can convert the fall chore of leaf-collecting into a short and pleasurable task by using a blower (which blows leaves into piles for collecting later) or a

Outdoor vacuuming

Blow fall leaves into a large pile, then change the setting and suck the leaves up, ready for disposal.

vacuum (which sucks leaves into a large pouch). Place all collected leaves into a wheelbarrow, then empty onto the compost heap to make useful leaf mold.

Some blowers are easily converted into leaf collectors at the flick of a switch or by fitting a vacuum tube attachment. Leaves sucked into the vacuum pass through a robust steel rotor blade that shreds them before they are packed into a leaf collector bag. When the bag is full, compost the shredded leaves or spread them as a mulch on your shrub and perennial borders.

A blower or powered leaf collector is a sound investment if you have a big garden or large areas of gravel (which makes raking very difficult). But be selective before buying: Compare models and ask for a demonstration of both electric and gasoline versions. Of the two, a gas-powered machine is more powerful and versatile—you don't have to negotiate obstacles

For the pruning season

A shredder is one of the speediest ways of disposing of clippings and prunings. The neatly shredded waste is ready for the compost heap or can be collected for easy disposal. Some models can be fitted with a collecting bag.

MULTIFUNCTIONAL TOOLS

If there isn't much space in your garden shed, consider investing in a multipurpose tool. This consists of a special handle onto which you can attach a whole variety of tool heads, including large and small rakes, hoes, brushes, cultivators, and so on. Handles are generally available in a range of sizes, from very long, to shorter ones suitable for hand tools. These allow you to choose the right model for your height.

and you can use it anywhere without worrying about a power cord. You will need to refill the fuel tank, though, so keep fuel in reserve and store it in an approved container. On the other hand, electric blowers are much quieter, making them a better choice if noise is an issue. Some blowers are very heavy, so be sure you can maneuver the tool with relative ease.

If you have a very large area to clear, consider a gas-powered, backpack vacuum. These have comfortable harnesses to reduce shoulder load, and rubber damping muffler to absorb engine vibration. There is little maintenance involved, provided you keep the machine free from mud, lubricate moving parts, spray

Small or large?

Many shredders allow you to adjust the cutting size. Fine shreds (left) make ideal mulch for your borders; use coarser shreds (right) in your compost, or for mulching larger areas.

metal areas with a water-repelling oil, and store the machine in a dry place. Drain the gasoline tank at the end of the season.

There are few more exasperating sights than a carefully gathered pile of leaves flying away in the wind before you have had a chance to dispose of it, so use your blower on a windless day or with the wind behind you. A word of warning, though: Keep it well away from your delicate plants. It discharges air at over 100 miles per hour and can badly damage any plants it encounters.

SHREDDERS

Pruning your shrubs and trees is a necessary and very satisfying business. But disposing of the cuttings can be time-consuming—which is where garden shredders come in. These machines make quick work of breaking down twigs and branches into much smaller, more manageable pieces that you can then transfer to your compost bin. They can also reduce fall leaves into leaf mold, which you can use as a mulch on your beds and borders.

Shredders range from smaller models, which will handle branches up to 1 inch in diameter, to large ones which can take branches of 3 inches. Electric models are useful if you have a medium to large garden, though if you have a lot of thick branches to tackle, consider hiring a gas-powered machine. When choosing a model to rent or buy, look for one that is stable during use; has a safety switch and cut-out in case of blockage; and a means of freeing blockages (such as reverse motion). Finally, consider your neighbors: choose a shredder with a quiet motor if you live in a heavily-populated area.

Most models are easy to use: Simply feed the woody prunings or leaves into a large funnel at one end of the machine, and the shredded material will exit from a chute at the other. Most garden debris is suitable for the shredder: vegetable waste, fall leaves, prunings, hedge, shrub and rose clippings, even hay and straw. But before you feed material through the shredder, check that there are no stray stones or soil, as these can blunt the cutting blades or block the machine.

Small pieces of wood or twigs can sometimes escape at high speed, so always wear eye goggles and thick gloves. Ear protectors are also recommended. You'll probably find that the machine clogs up from time to time; remember to disconnect the power and wait for the moving parts to stop before trying to fix it.

"A garden has a curious innocent way of consuming cash while all the time you are under the illusion that you are spending nothing."

ESTHER MEYNELL, WRITER AND BIOGRAPHER

Water features

Water adds a completely new dimension to a garden—bringing with it life, light, color, and movement. Whether you have in mind a quiet pool or a trickling fountain, there are assorted tools to help create and maintain your garden oasis.

Water gardens are irresistible and endlessly versatile. Even the smallest garden pool invites children and adults to peer into its mysterious depths. Spouts and fountains add sparkle and splash to their surroundings, while quiet pools also have their own serene romance, reflecting the sky, rippling in the breeze, and teeming with wildlife.

Design

Water features can take almost any shape or form you choose, from cutting-edge, contemporary designs to the most traditional and formal. There are plenty of starter kits and self-contained water features available, which make installing a simple pond or trickling fountain an easy project, or you could use any waterproof materials that take your fancy to make one. Try adding your own creative touches—perhaps some shell or pebble designs, glass chips, or underwater lighting.

Pump power

Moving water features need a good pump to propel them. Submersible pumps with a low voltage are generally simple to install. The size will depend upon the height (or lift) that the water reaches above the surface of your feature and the amount of water that will be flowing through it (the flow rate). A small feature may require a pump with a flow rate of about 120 gallons per hour, while a large fountain or spout may need as much as 270 gallons per hour. There are also a variety of hose fittings and connectors available, some fitted with filters, and some able to adjust the flow of water.

Planting

Think carefully about the plants in and around your water feature and try to choose the right combination of easy-care aquatic plants so the

The water works

Dirty-water pumps (far left) will help to clear muddy water There is also a wide range of extendable pond-cleaning tools (center and left), ideal for skimming and cutting back weeds and for removing fish

Clearing the waters

Pool-cleaning equipment (left and above) varies from the most basic to the most advanced, but a simple skimmer, net, or leaf rake is sufficient to keep the surface tidy. If you have to get in, a pair of waders will keep you warm and dry.

to help prevent overgrown and murky ponds. These have no sharp edges to hurt fish.

Liners

Most ponds are made with one of two types of liner: preformed rigid liners, often made in regular shapes and depths, or flexible sheets that can be used to fit almost any shape. Underlays are recommended as extra insurance for these liners, and repair kits can be bought to fix minor damage.

Clear water

Healthy, clean water is essential for your water feature to look good and for your fish and plants to thrive. You can buy test sets that will measure the acidity, nitrite, and ammonia levels.

Filters can be bought to fit onto pumps or to bury alongside your water feature. They may incorporate a built-in UV-Clarifier, or this can be bought separately. UV-light destroys the green, single-celled, waterborne algae that makes garden ponds murky and unattractive. As no chemicals are used, there is no danger of pollution or over-treatment of the water, and sensitive plant and pond life is not affected.

Manual pumps are available to suck up solids such as silt, leaves, and fish droppings, and to pump it onto your flower beds as fertilizer. You can also buy powered vacuum cleaners, which are expensive, but are wonderful at removing sludge, algae, and leaves from large garden ponds. They usually come with a long suction hose to allow you to reach all parts of your pond.

Effective, safe, and fully biodegradable, pads containing lavender stalks and barley straw, effective natural algaecides, are a natural treatment for algae in ponds of all sizes. Place one in an area of good water circulation. (Pads will float and may be tied just below the surface with string and a stone). Add another after 4 months, simply leaving the first pad to rot away. They are not recommended in systems without forced water circulation, however, as there may be a shortage of oxygen in the water.

Pond cover nets will also save you work in the fall, when your water may be swamped by a blanket of dropped leaves.

pond becomes largely self-sustaining. Specially designed baskets are handy to plant in and are often shaped to follow the contours of pools.

There are also more flexible, fabric "aquaplanters" available that hold in aquatic compost and roots

Tools for transport

Whether you are harvesting fruit and vegetables, building a new garden structure, planting containers, or weeding your borders, you'll need some carryalls and other hauling equipment to help you move materials around your garden.

If you have a small yard, you'll probably get away with a bucket and a basket, but a wheelbarrow or cart is a must-have for those with large gardens or who regularly move heavy loads from one part of the garden to another.

WHEELBARROWS

Since the wheelbarrow was invented in China in around A.D. 200, it has revolutionized the transport of soil, plants, and a thousand other things, allowing us to move weights far greater than we could carry by hand. It is simple in design, consisting of little more than a pair of levers fixed to a large wheel.

It is unlikely that you have ever wondered how a wheelbarrow works, but how does it bear a load far greater than you can carry? Most of the weight, when

Holding and hauling
A basket (above) is perfect for moving small, lightweight items around the garden; use a wheelbarrow (right) for bulkier materials.

Look for a wheelbarrow with a pneumatic tire, at least 4 inches wide, which will absorb shocks without jolting and which rides comfortably over a bumpy surface; a frame of reinforced tubular steel; a deep, high-capacity steel or polypropylene tray; and a projecting metal "nose" to make tipping easier.

you lift the handles, is transferred to a wheel that acts as a fulcrum. Indeed, the mass pressing down on the wheel actually aids forward movement. With just one wheel, the wheelbarrow is extremely maneuverable. It allows you to twist, turn, and negotiate obstacles, even along narrow paths.

The first wheelbarrows designed for gardens were heavy, wooden carts with metal-rimmed wheels. These wheelbarrows never wore out, but what a noise they made when trundled over uneven stone or concrete surfaces. You can still buy old-fashioned wooden barrows, but you may prefer a modern, lighter version. Whatever you use your wheelbarrow for— moving manure, soil, weeds, stones, logs, leaves, grass cuttings, prunings, or bags of cement—it's important to load it on a level surface. You can double the capacity of some models by fitting an extension top. This is invaluable for collecting leaves in the fall.

To keep your wheelbarrow in peak working order, wipe the tray out each time you use it—you may need to use a wire brush if mud is really caked on—and turn it upside-down to drain it. Lubricate the wheel fittings once a season and check all the nuts and screws on a yearly basis, tightening if necessary. It is also worth pumping up the tire from time to time.

THE HISTORY OF WHEELBARROWS

The wheelbarrow has been around for millennia in China. An inventor named Ko Yu is credited with the idea for the first wheelbarrow, possibly around the first century B.C. It has been used ever since for carrying all sorts of items, from agricultural materials and war equipment (the tool was a favorite with ancient Chinese armies), to human beings.

It wasn't until the eleventh or twelfth century A.D. that the wheelbarrow first appeared in Europe—the earliest known Western depiction is in a window at Chartres Cathedral, France, dated around A.D. 1220. Farmers soon realized that wheelbarrows were a cheap, efficient substitute for animals.

Today, tractors and harvesters are used to do most of the hard work on agricultural land, but the wheelbarrow is still important in the domestic garden shed.

Through the ages

Early models had a wheel in the center of the wooden frame; later, the wheel was placed at the front of the frame instead. The materials have evolved, too: for centuries wood was favored for the tray, frame, and even the wheel, but gradually this was replaced by longer-lasting metal frames, metal or plastic trays, and pneumatic rubber tires.

Folding wheelbarrows

Traditional wheelbarrows are quite bulky and take up a lot of storage space. Some manufacturers make a folding wheelbarrow as an alternative. This model has a canvas tray and a lightweight frame, and can be hung from a hook in the wall when not in use.

METAL MODELS

Metal wheelbarrows come in many shapes and sizes, all of which should be stored covered. Some trays are galvanized; others are made of a reinforced polypropylene tray that's unaffected by temperatures from -50° to 138°F. This material won't dent, buckle, or become brittle in frigid conditions.

The strongest frames are wrought from a single length of tubular steel with two welded cross members. When it comes to wheels, choose from solid or tubeless pneumatic tires (filled with compressed air). For the smoothest ride, buy a wheelbarrow with a broad pneumatic tire (about 4 inches thick) and "needle" bearings.

How much a wheelbarrow can carry depends on its size. Unless you have weak wrists, don't buy a model with less than 20 gallons' capacity. After all, you don't have to fill it so full that you stagger with it. The deeper it is, the more useful it will be to you.

A wheelbarrow with a tool box accessory at the base of the handles will provide permanent storage for your pruning shears, trowels, string, and knives.

FOLDING-FRAMED WHEELBARROWS

If you're stuck for space and don't have room for a rigid-framed wheelbarrow, opt for a folding version that can be hung on a wall. Sturdy and well-balanced, its galvanized frame supports a deep tray of tough, tear-resistant fabric and a chunky, solid wheel takes the strain. It's easy to push when piled high with garden trash and as versatile as a conventional barrow: It can even be used for carting logs and bricks.

CARTS

With larger trays or pans than a wheelbarrow, carts are well-balanced for moving heavy loads. They are strong enough to withstand rough use year after year, and, being two-wheeled, they can't accidentally topple sideways. What's more, the flat bottom makes for easy stacking. They are also simple to empty: Simply tip them forward. There are two kinds: One has a bolt-free polyethylene pan that snaps onto and off a

Garden dollies

Constructed from pine or UV-protected polypropylene, and fitted with hard-wearing castors, plant dollies are the easy and sensible answer to moving heavy patio tubs and pots, or bags of compost or cement. Some kinds have enclosed wheel housings for extra strength.

tubular, aluminum alloy frame for emptying. The other has a galvanized steel tray, an epoxy-coated, tubular steel frame, spoked wheels with bearings, and a large pan.

Four-wheeled carts vary in size enormously. One type, made from rugged polypropylene, has a large central compartment, molded tool clips to hold long-handled tools and an adjustable handle which folds to form a comfortable seat.

SACK TRUCKS

Originally, millers used sack trucks to transport corn and flour, and the name stuck. The big advantage of a sack truck over a cart is that you do not have to lift the load. You simply ease the base plate under the object you wish to lift and pull back on the handles. Most base plates are flat, but some have right-angled sides to stop the load from slipping.

When using a sack truck at a 45 degree angle from the ground, the leverage is such that you can transport

Save your back

For moving really heavy items, such as large containers, a sack truck will come in useful, as you can slide the footplate under the pot instead of lifting the pot onto the truck.

ROLL-OUT PATHWAYS

Walking or transporting loads across rain-drenched lawns and borders in foul weather is totally inadvisable. Wet soil is easily compressed, and its fragile, open structure quickly destroyed. However, you can keep on the move by laying a 12-inch-wide portable path made from tough, interlocking, molded, polypropylene slats. It's the sensible way to keep working during showers.

The roll-out pathway has other uses, too. Lay it alongside a row of peas or beans to allow you to pick pods on the wettest day of summer without soiling your shoes, or compacting and damaging soggy soil. When you've finished with it, hose it down, roll it up, and store it.

exceptionally heavy loads, albeit slowly. Indeed, a sack truck is ideal for moving large, heavy, planted containers and tubs, rock garden stone, peat bales, and bags of compost, gravel, and cement. When you deposit the load, simply ease it forward slightly to release the base plate.

STEPLADDER TRUCK CART

This variation on the sack truck is a useful combination of a two-step ladder and truck that saves you looking for a box to stand on when you need to move out-of-reach objects. An occasional squirt of oil to keep the wheels from squeaking is all you need to remember to do.

BUCKETS, BAGS, AND SHEETS

Whether it's made from galvanized steel, rubber, or heavy-duty plastic, a bucket is a gardener's ally when tidying up borders. While weeding, it's easy to first fill

All-purpose tools

No garden shed is complete without a bucket
or two, either of galvanized steel (far left),
plastic (left), or even rubber; use them to
carry or mix materials.

a bucket with weeds and then empty it into a wheelbarrow. A bucket is also indispensable for mixing fertilizer, baling out a pond, and for filling with soap solution to wash dirty pots.

You will find many uses for a capacious bag made from durable, woven polypropylene: Have it beside you when weeding a border or pruning shrubs.

A tough, waterproof sheet has similar beneficial uses. Spread it out where you are working in the garden, and throw weeds and other garbage on it. When full, gather it up and add the contents to your compost bin or trash pile.

BUCKETS

As Jeff Taylor says in his book, *Tools of the Earth*: "No garden can get by without a bucket or three. It is among the most versatile, ignored, and generally abused tools. It gets tossed about and dropped, filled with all sorts of unpleasant things, and left out in the elements. All other garden tools get a spring clean and a winter rest, but never the bucket. It hauls ash from the wood stove to the ash can and fills up with rain or snow in between."

Whether you prefer a galvanized bucket with a thick wire handle and double-locked side seams; a heavy-duty, plastic builder's bucket with a lip for pouring; or one with a rope handle, the heavier the bucket, the less likely it is to be blown around in gusty winds. It's even more useful when calibrated in gallons and quarts. If you decide to buy a galvanized steel bucket, examine it closely, making sure the handles and base are securely attached to the body and that the seams are well-sealed. When you've finished using the bucket, store it in a dry place.

Top-quality plastic buckets are lighter than steel but just as strong and rust-free. They also tend to cost much less than their metal counterparts.

BAGS

The choice of bags is enormous: One version, made from strong, waterproof nylon with webbing handles, stands up for filling, but is easily collapsed for storage and transport. A family of bags you'll want to become familiar with are made from tough, nontear, woven

>good ideas

Attempting to hold a bag open with one hand while you shovel leaves, soil, or other debris into it with the other can be a trying experience. So manufacturers have come up with an ingenious design for a self-opening and collapsing bag. While in use, it stays open for easy filling and emptying (you can also angle the bag to make this task even simpler), and when you've finished, it collapses into a neat, flat disk for easy storage and transportation.

Versatile garden sheets

These are perfect for collecting weeds and garden trash (above). If you are collecting a lot of material, such as when hedge trimming, sheets are available that join together with bamboo canes (right); once you have finished your task, remove the canes and use the handles at each corner (far right) to gather up the cuttings and dispose of them.

polyethylene. Some are self-supporting, with a huge capacity; others, which also stand up by themselves, have flexible inserts. Many come with robust nylon handles and all wipe clean.

A clever hybrid between a wheelbarrow and a bag is the refuse cart—a large polyethylene bag supported by a wheeled and galvanized steel frame. Simply fill the bag and wheel it to your compost heap. An extra benefit is that you can put it in the trunk of your car for an easy trip to the garbage dump.

SHEETS

Woven polyethylene sheets are invaluable for collecting weeds and leaf litter while you're working on a border. Spread a sheet out on the grass or pathway and throw all your border garbage onto it. When you've built up a sizable heap, grab the four carrying handles and fold them into the middle. Dump the contents onto your compost heap.

An attractive alternative to a plastic sheet is a carrier made of heavy-duty, oiled, green canvas. Edged with natural burlap, it is tough enough to cope with most garden waste and less likely to get punctured by a stray twig than the plastic versions. If you're taking a load of garbage in your trunk to the dump, tie the

handles together. Keep sheets free from mud by hosing them down, drying them, and storing them until their next use.

TRUGS

This lovely old-fashioned word describes long, light, shallow baskets traditionally crafted from veneers of wood. The body is usually made from willow, the handles and trim from sweet chestnut. Generally there are three sizes that you can choose from. The smallest (8 x 24 inches) is ideal for carrying small tools; the next size up (11 x 19 inches) is perfect for kitchen garden produce; and the largest (14 x 25 inches) is favored by gardeners who spend many hours in the garden. The shallow cradle of all trugs means that you can carry cut flowers indoors without squashing their delicate petals.

Also known as the tub trug, the two-handled trug is strong, flexible, and made from recycled plastic. Use it to gather weeds and other garbage, to carry plants and tools, to mix compost, and to scoop organic matter.

BASKETS

Wicker (willow), bamboo, wire, and rush—these lightweight materials make the perfect container for newly-harvested fruit, vegetables, and of course, flowers for your table. For carrying heavy crops, use a high-sided wooden or canvas fruit-picker's basket. Wire baskets are handy as they allow air to circulate around fruit and vegetables, and are also impervious to mold.

THE MAKING OF TRUGS

When harvesting flowers, you need a lightweight, shallow container in which to lay the blooms so that they won't get squashed. The ideal tool for the job is the trug, which was invented in the 1820s by Thomas Smith of Herstmonceux, a village in southern England.

The trug takes its name from an Anglo-Saxon word, "trog," which was a wooden vessel, shaped like a round coracle boat, used by farmers to measure grain and liquids. Thomas Smith redesigned the historic trog to produce a lighter-weight basket, made of sweet chestnut and willow wood. The trug soon became a favorite of gardeners around the world.

Traditionally-made trugs are still available today, in durable chestnut, lightweight willow, plywood, birch veneer, and other natural materials such as plaited rush. A well-crafted handmade trug is a better investment than a plastic imitation: Kept dry, it will last for years—and it looks so at home on the kitchen table or in the garden shed.

Handmade trugs

To make traditional Sussex trugs, skilled craftspeople today employ virtually the same techniques as Thomas Smith would have used nearly 200 years ago.

1 **CUTTING THE SLATS** Lengths of willow are hand-shaven into very fine strips of about an ⅛ inch thick, which will make the slats for the trug.

2 **MAKING THE FRAME** Pieces of chestnut are cut into lengths for the rim and handle, which are then steamed to make them flexible. Next, the wood is bent around a frame to make a hoop, which is held with small tacks. After the handle and rim have been nailed together, the willow slats are steamed and curved, then nailed to the frame.

3 **FINISHING TOUCHES** The slats are trimmed down to create a smooth edge.

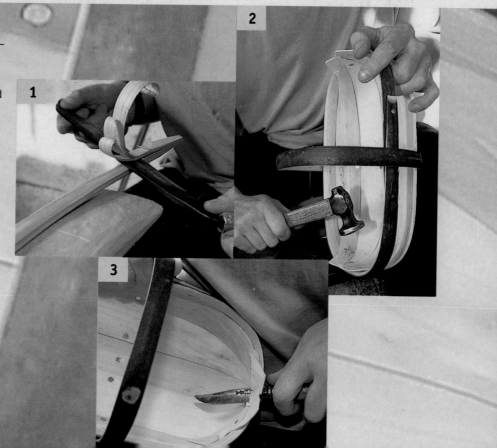

Composting

There are few more satisfying tasks in gardening than converting organic waste into nutrient-rich humus. It's not only free to make and environmentally responsible, but its also the soil's life blood. Weeds, grass cuttings, soft prunings, plant remains, peelings, and other kitchen waste—whatever you recycle—the end product is similar. If you make an effort to keep it warm, moist, and aerated, your reward will be a crumbly, black material teeming with worms and beneficial microbes that are excellent for conditioning your soil. The humus improves the structure of all soils, opening the texture of heavy clay soils (thereby aiding drainage and root growth), helping sandy soils to retain water, and adding vital nutrients. The result is a more productive garden.

To make a compost heap you can simply pile waste green materials into a corner of the garden where they will eventually decompose. But the most efficient way to process green waste is to put it in a compost bin that keeps it under the right conditions in which micro-organisms break it down into humus.

Aim to spend a little time blending fibrous, carbon-rich materials such as dry leaves or straw, which give

COMPOSTING THROUGH THE AGES

It can't have escaped early humans' attention that wherever they emptied their bladders, the vegetation grew exceptionally well. Patches of very lush grassland would crop up where ground was fertilized in this way.

Around 1000 years ago it was common practice to add blood, including that from humans, to dung, wood ash, manure and other materials that rot. In the late nineteenth century, the almost sanctified habit of composting was eclipsed by the introduction of artificial fertilizers. Thankfully, this short-sightedness was brief and compost-heap devotees continued thereafter to perfect their art.

The birth of the twentieth century found Sir Albert Howard stating that the best compost is made by mixing three parts plant waste to one part manure. A century later, it's still a highly respected formula.

> **"Everyone has a theory about composting. For the kitchen refuse I keep a big brown pot on the windowsill behind the sink, and into it go all the tea leaves, apple peel, onion skins, and coffee grounds."**
> MARGERY FISH, GARDENING WRITER (1888–1969)

your heap "body," with softer nitrogen-rich waste, such as grass cuttings, fruit and vegetable scraps, and old, unwanted garden plants. Keep a healthy balance: If there's too much carbon, compost will take a long time to break down, and conversely, if there's an excess of soft-stemmed material, it will become a slimy, airless mess.

The larger the bin, the more heat it retains, and the quicker compost will decompose. If you have enough space, try to keep two adjoining bins: one filled with compost left to finish rotting, and the other in the process of being filled.

COMPOST BINS

Your compost bin should be at least 65 gallons in volume with a lid to keep materials warm and actively fermenting. There should also be a door at the base— or a removable side—for digging out well-rotted compost. If there is no door, tilt the bin to remove the finest compost (usually from the bottom of the heap).

Wooden bins These are normally made of preserved softwood panels at least ¾ inch thick; the container should not be less than 3 feet square and deep. Some models have interlocking sides to make it easy to remove compost.

Plastic Usually made from recycled heavy-duty polypropylene, plastic is tough and durable and won't crack in subzero temperatures or perish when it's hot. Most kinds have wide, easy-opening doors, either hinged or sliding, and a full-sized lid for easy filling.

Wire mesh Easy to make, plastic-coated wire mesh is fixed to a framework of four preserved posts. Insulate the bin with polystyrene sheets or thick cardboard to keep the wind from cooling the heap.

Plastic fertilizer bags Moist leaves and other finely shredded waste will rot down within these small bags. When full, tie the bag tightly at the top and make a

WHICH COMPOST BIN IS BEST FOR YOU?

When choosing a compost bin, take into account the size and style of your garden. If you have just a compact garden, opt for a small, discreet model; larger gardens can support a bigger bin. Plastic bins (top) retain heat efficiently and are easily transported around the garden. Chicken wire composters (center) are simple to construct and a good choice for the budget-conscious. Wooden, interlocking bins (below) may come with a removable front for easy access to the compost.

few ventilation holes in the side with a garden fork. Store the bags in a cool, wind-free part of the garden until the contents have broken down into crumbly black humus and are ready for use.

Compost tumbler This unique device is a plastic bin mounted on a sturdy galvanized-steel frame that you turn daily to force oxygen through the waste. This stimulates microbes to break down organic matter, which, in turn, raises the temperature to 120° F and causes compost to decompose rapidly. So in summer, finely-shredded organic waste can be converted into humus in as little as five weeks. After processing the

COMPOSTING MATERIALS

Good compost-making ingredients include fruit and vegetable scraps, straw and hay, dead flowers and bedding plants, soft prunings, pet bedding, tea bags and coffee grounds, vegetable plant remains, young hedge clippings, wood ash, cardboard, paper towels, and perennial weeds (except for persistent horrors like couch grass and ground elder).

Never compost cat litter, dog feces, disposable diapers, meat, or fish, as these will attract vermin. Glossy magazines, and coal and coke ash will not decompose. Also avoid onions infected with white rot, potatoes with blight, brassicas diseased with clubroot, or weeds that have already gone to seed.

TIPS FOR SUCCESS

Activators A compost activator speeds up the rotting process and is usually found in manure, artificial fertilizers, microbes, and enzymes. Comfrey leaves, grass cuttings, and young weeds will also kick-start beneficial bacteria into breaking down the heap.

Good insulation No matter what sort of compost container you choose, it must retain heat. Decomposition stops if cold winds cool fermenting

compost you can either spread it around the garden and dig it in, or add it to a compost bin where it will break down into finer particles. A simpler version of the compost tumbler is a big hollow plastic ball with a lid on the top, which you can roll around to keep turning the compost inside.

Making a simple compost bin

1 Using a large, heavy mallet or hammer, drive four sturdy fence posts into the ground to form a square. These will help to stabilize the bin.

2 Wrap galvanized chicken wire around the posts. You'll need about 12 feet of 36-inch-wide, 1-inch wire mesh to make a container 3 feet in diameter. Nongalvanized wire is less weather-resistant and won't last as long.

3 Fold back 3 or 4 inches at each end of the wire, to make a clean edge that won't easily snag.

4 Secure the wire to the posts with nails. Fold the nail back on itself, using a hammer, for extra strength.

5 Attach the two ends of the chicken wire together using some heavy wire. You may need pliers for this job.

6 To remove the finished compost, simply disconnect the wire on one side of the bin. Alternatively, for even easier access, consider constructing a gate on one side of the bin.

Green gardening

Composting is central to organic gardening. Other eco-friendly practices include installing a lacewing chamber (right), which helps these beneficial insects survive winter safely. You can also encourage mason wasps—essential for pollinating fruit trees—to live in your trees with a specially designed shelter (far right) and nesting tubes.

compost. A thick sheet of polystyrene is one of the most efficient insulators—in fact some compost bins are made from it! It's usually sandwiched between two layers of heavy-duty plastic to prevent the polystyrene from cracking. Tough polypropylene or wooden panels, not less than ¾ inch wide, also effectively keep heat where you want it—breaking down plant tissue.

Siting the bin Warmth and moisture are necessary for making good garden compost, so position the container in a sheltered spot where icy winds cannot cool it. There should also be room next to it for a wheelbarrow and for stacking materials before you load them into the bin. Choose a well-drained area of soil for the bin to sit on, as you want worms and microbes to enter the heap. You may also want to position your bin so that you cannot see it from the windows of your house.

Maintain the decomposition process You should aim to turn your pile about once a month to speed the natural breakdown of the organic matter. If you don't turn it regularly, the composting process will slow down, and you may notice an unpleasant smell beginning to emanate from your pile.

A standard four-tined garden fork will do an adequate job of turning your compost pile, but you will find a compost or manure fork more helpful; the five or six more closely-spaced tines grab onto the plant material with greater efficiency, causing less to fall through the prongs.

The enthusiastic compostor might want to consider investing in an aerator (a blade at the end of a long handle), which helps to introduce oxygen to the pile, and a special, long compost thermometer that allows you to take temperature readings at the center of the pile easily.

CREATING A COMPOST HEAP

Start by covering the base with a 4-inch layer of coarse prunings or brassica stems to help air circulate through the heap. Add an 8-inch layer of mixed coarse and fine waste. Avoid thick slabs of grass which trap air and turn smelly. Cover the compost with a granular or liquid activator. Water dry materials or they won't rot. Continue in this fashion, adding 8-inch layers of compost treated with activator, until you have filled the container. Throughout this period, keep the lid on to keep rain from soaking the compost and stopping its breakdown.

Within a week or so, the heap will heat up. When it cools, turn materials with a fork. Aim to work the cooler and less-decomposed on the outside of the heap, into the middle. When the heap reheats, air introduced when mixing materials will stimulate microbes to continue feasting. Turn the heap again. Finally, when it no longer heats up, leave it to finish composting.

You will know the decomposition process is complete and the compost is ready to use when you have a rich, crumbly brownish-black material. Add a 1- to 2-inch layer of compost to your flower beds each year to keep the soil healthy and fertile. It also makes a good mulch around newly planted flowers and shrubs, and an efficient fertilizer for your lawn. When using compost on your borders, you may want to sift it first with a garden sieve to remove any larger, undecomposed debris.

7

Working Safely

Protective clothing

Do you watch what you wear when you are gardening? Probably not—provided you are comfortable, your clothes are loose, and you can bend and twist without getting caught up. Few of us actually buy gardening clothes. Instead we tend to recycle old shirts, sweaters, and long pants that have lost their respectability. When you're digging in manure, weeding, or planting, it's only your neighbors who can see you, and they are probably similarly attired. However, some items of clothing should not be worn when old and worn out, such as boots, gloves, waterproof jackets, fleece sweatshirts, and hats. Be careful never to wear jewelry, loose-fitting clothes, or long hair down, as they might get caught in equipment.

But no matter how experienced a gardener you are, you should be aware of the elements to which you are exposed when gardening. On a day-to-day basis, you will need to evaluate how best to protect yourself from a variety of hazards. These may include exposure to the burning effects of the sun, the unpleasant dampness of the rain, the risk of contact with insects and irritating plants, and the cuts and bruises you may receive through using your tools.

Before starting a job, think carefully about what clothing and footwear you will need to accomplish it safely. You should always protect your eyes with safety glasses when mowing, pruning, trimming hedges, and using a chain saw. Similarly, safeguard your hands with thornproof gloves when pruning hooked rose stems. Wear long-sleeved gloves for rearranging water plants in ponds and strap on kneeling pads to cushion your knees from sharp stones and damp soil.

"Oh, Adam was a gardener, and God who made him sees
That half a proper gardener's work is done upon his knees."
RUDYARD KIPLING, NOVELIST AND POET (1865–1936)

Head gear
A cap (left) or a broad-brimmed hat (right) will shield your head and neck from the sun, and help to prevent burning and sunstroke.

LOOKING AFTER YOUR FEET
Never wear old shoes in the garden; their soles are likely to be thin and won't offer much in the way of protection from nails, thorns, and other sharp objects. Wounds can then become infected with tetanus—for which you should be regularly immunized.

Unless your shoes are made of tough leather or rubber, they are unlikely to be waterproof. Wet feet are not only unpleasant but may cause you to suffer from a host of ailments. To garden comfortably, hour after hour, you will need two sorts of boots: Wellingtons, and boots made from leather, rubber, or PVC. Your choice of which to wear will depend on the day's activities and tools you intend to use.

WELLINGTON BOOTS
These are ideal for short periods of muddy work after heavy rains have saturated lawns and borders. They should fit snugly around your feet and legs, and have reinforced soles to protect your feet from the sharp edge of a blade when you are digging or using implements like lawn edgers.

If you're working for several hours, short-length Wellingtons are better than full-length ones, which may rub your legs and make them sore. If you wade into a pond wearing Wellingtons, check frequently

Mud, mud, glorious mud
Wellington boots really come into their own when the ground is wet. Look for a high-grip tread pattern to provide a better slip-free foothold.

that the water level is below the top of your boots—there's nothing worse than damp feet!

Long PVC or rubber Wellingtons should be lined for comfort, and have reinforced seams for strength and a cushioned sole. Some have a steel shank for added support and an adjustable strap at the top. There are several types: One very popular form, if you suffer from cold feet, is a snug-fitting PVC boot. Plain-styled with a square toe, it has a textile-ribbed or padded rubber and laced collar and comes complete with a textile inner lining that will keep your feet warm in the coldest weather.

CLOGS, SHOES, AND ANKLE BOOTS
Very convenient and easy to wear, waterproof clogs, slip-on shoes, and ankle boots are best used for brief dashes into the garden. Keep them by the back door for wearing when emptying the garbage, feeding the birds, or popping into the garden shed. Natural rubber clogs are reliable and enjoyable to wear,

At the end of the day, hang your mucky boots on a boot rack. Brush off the caked mud once it has dried.

especially if they have cork insoles and cotton lining to absorb perspiration. A reinforced area under the ball of the foot makes digging a painless exercise. Incidentally, over rough ground, closed-backed clogs are easier to keep on than open-backed ones.

If you intend to spend only few moments on a saturated lawn or border, you can put on overboots rather than Wellingtons. Strong, waterproof and easily slipped on overshoes, they are made from natural latex and have reinforced soles.

LEATHER AND PVC BOOTS

Whether they are made from leather or PVC, boots are more comfortable than basic Wellingtons and can be worn for considerably longer periods. If you have a largish garden in which you spend a lot of time walking from one job to the next, a strong, waterproof pair of boots is essential, particularly if you have uneven patches of ground in your plot over which you could stumble.

When buying full-grained, lace-up leather boots (which have an extremely long life), make sure they have thick and hard-wearing soles to cushion you against sharp stones, nails, and other objects. They should also have a moisture-wicking liner (which

removes perspiration from your feet), a flexible but tough mid-sole, and a lightweight carbon rubber outer-sole.

Alternatively, opt for lightweight "breathable" boots made from suede and waterproof Gore-tex. Steel toe caps are not necessary unless you are cutting heavy branches which might land awkwardly. Another type of waterproof boot has PVC soles and Velcro fastenings—so you can take them off much more quickly than you can untie boot laces.

Should you need to work in deep water, slip on a pair of medium-weight thigh-, waist-, or chest-length PVC waders. Textile-lined, they come with a reinforced ankle, heel, and toe.

CHEST, ARMS, AND LEGS

You must not forget, when tackling a multitude of gardening challenges, to respect the weather and dress accordingly. To enjoy these tasks, it's important that you stay dry and warm during rain and chilly winds—while feeling cool when the sun heats up the garden. Sweat—which is inevitably produced by vigorous

Slip-ons

Natural rubber slip-ons (right) are easy to step into and out of when you're coming and going from the garden. Boots that fit over shoes (far right) are also good for running in and out of the house.

Bibs and cushions

Keep your clothes clean by wearing an apron over the top (far left); pockets are a handy place to stash hand tools and other accessories when not in use. Knee pads (left) will cushion your delicate knee joints and also prevent slipping.

exercise—should not build up. If it does, and you stop working, it may "ice" the skin and trigger aches and pains. It's important to wear clothes that "wick away" moisture immediately. That means using a three-layer system.

First layer Worn next to the skin, Polartec—based on polyester—absorbs less than half of one percent of its weight of water. Close-fitting shirts and pants in this material are a pleasure to wear, pulling moisture away from your body and leaving it warm and dry.

Second layer This consists of a high-loft, fleece sweatshirt that not only traps warm, dry air close to your body, but allows moisture to evaporate. Most have a high double collar, front pockets, and a drawstring hem with locking toggle.

Third layer This top layer should be a jacket made from breathable but waterproof and windproof Goretex that retains body heat but allows body water vapor to escape. Make sure that the version you buy has taped seams, articulated elbows for easy movement, a peaked roll-away hood with side drainage channels, adjustable outer cuffs, and large pockets. It should also be machine-washable.

Aprons Why soil a shirt or pants with potting compost or other staining substances when you can wear an apron to keep yourself clean and warm on a cool day? Knee-length bib-types are best, made of polyester and cotton, or denim, with one or more large pockets for carrying string and hand tools.

Waders and yard boots

If you have a large pond in your garden (or are partial to fishing), you may want to invest in a pair of thigh-length waders (far left). Oiled, leather boots (left) are generally built to last; this particular pair just slips on, a real time-saver

Child's play

Encouraging a budding young gardener to develop his or her creative talents is a joyful duty, and one made much easier and safer by some of the specially-designed tools that are available today.

It's heartening when a child—curious and interested in what you're doing in the yard—wants to join in and help.

The first step is to give junior a well-drained plot on which to grow anything that appeals to him or her—from showy sunflowers and nasturtiums, to perennials, vegetables, and fruit. Thankfully, a few enterprising companies have designed good, lightweight tools for children, which should not break if they are misused. It's probably best to avoid giving youngsters adult-sized spades, forks, hoes, or rakes, as these will be too large and heavy, and may prove hazardous.

Safe digging tools

Initially, it's a good idea for an adult to dig the patch of ground to make it easier for the child to cultivate. But then there is a variety of tools to help youngsters to take over.

Few garden tasks are more exciting for a child than planting perennials and bedding plants that grow and flower quickly. Make it easy and satisfying with a tough, plastic, well-designed hand fork.

You can also plant bulbs with a hand fork, but it's easier to set them with a trowel. Mark the blade in inches so the child knows exactly how deep to dig a hole for small or large bulbs.

The best spades—which can also be used as shovels—have durable fiberglass-reinforced plastic, shield-shaped blades with wooden pole-shaped handles.

Learning the fun way

Giving your children projects with rewarding outcomes—such as proudly eating their own produce or enjoying fast-growing annual flowers—will fire their imaginations.

Clockwise from far left: Equip your kids with fun clothing; bright Wellingtons, preferably with reinforced seams and, importantly, with a high-grip tread. There are kids' versions of most adult tools, including rakes, brooms, spades, wheelbarrows, and watering cans.

Clean and rake it up

Essential for leveling and crumbling soil, and covering seedlings, there are heavy-duty plastic and fiberglass rakes with 10 tines and wooden handles. You can also buy children's leaf rakes, replicating in miniature a flexible 12-tined adult version. The fiberglass and plastic teeth effectively aerate a lawn by removing thatch from grass blades.

It is also worth buying a broom, so your child can enjoy sweeping a path, patio, or terrace. Choose a stiff-bristled model with a small head and short handle.

To help children develop a passion for gardening, stress the fun aspect—buy a lightweight wheelbarrow and offer them a ride in it! One of the best has a red-painted 6 gallon tray on a matte-black frame, with a polypropylene wheel, and safety-grip handles that help balance the load.

Plantings

The faster seeds germinate, the more they can hold a child's attention. Growing mustard and watercress is an excellent first project. Take a pot, fill it with compost, and moisten it. Sprinkle mustard seeds thickly over it and sow the watercress three days later. Mist the seeds. Place the pot in a clear plastic bag and move it to a warm, dark place. When, after a week or so, seedlings are 2 inches high, transfer them to a sunny spot to grow.

In early fall, buy prepared hyacinth bulbs. Set them close together in bowls of bulb fiber. Water them and put them in a cool, dark place to form roots. When, after six weeks or so, leaves are 1–2 inches high with embryo blooms showing, move the bowls to a sunny spot.

Fuel a child's enthusiasm for gardening early, and they will be avid gardeners for life.

PROTECTING YOUR HANDS

Without gloves to guard us from icy winds that numb fingers and crack skin, gardening would not be the pleasant, comfortable pastime it is. Besides comfort, they do a very good job of protecting us from cruel rose thorns and manure that often harbors tetanus.

There are waterproof gloves to keep us warm and dry, wool mittens that cover all but fingertips, tough thornproof gloves for tackling vicious shrubs, and long-sleeved versions for working in ponds.

THE GLOVE TEST

All gloves should be strong enough to withstand repeated encounters with an enemy of barbed shrubs and stony soil. They should also be flexible and sensitive enough for us to carry out nimble tasks. We tend to buy gloves for different purposes: light weeding, handling rough objects, pruning, and keeping our hands dry when it's wet out.

FABRIC GLOVES

Cotton, jersey, and canvas gloves are inexpensive and ideal for keeping hands clean on a dry day—as hands can also breathe. The best have PVC dots for a better grip. Look for a clute-cut glove in which the palm side is a single piece of material. Fabric gloves are machine washable. If you wear them when it's wet out, they will soak up water, causing your hands to freeze.

VINYL GLOVES

These are hard-wearing and waterproof, but sufficiently flexible and close-fitting for sowing seeds or taking cuttings. Vinyl gloves have a warm, soft cotton lining, and they won't clog with dirt.

STORING GLOVES SAFELY

When you have finished using them, make a habit of storing them in the same place every time. Coming in pairs, it's exasperating to lose one: you won't do this if you buy a brand that can be snapped together when not in use. They will serve you well as long as you wash them occasionally to remove the dirt that tends to accumulate in the finger tips. When dry, store them flat in a warm, dry place. Never stuff them in pockets, which will ruin their shape.

THE FINER POINTS...

Seamless...
Choose gloves that have a flexible, seamless back. They should be comfortable and roomy—too tight and they will restrict blood flow and your fingers will stay cold.

Leather-palmed...
These should have a safety cuff for extra wrist protection.

Double-sewn thumbs...
Ensure that tough, hard-wearing gloves have double-sewn thumbs with extra thick material at wear points.

POND GLOVES

If you have a skin problem or a cut that hasn't healed, never plunge your bare hands or arms into a pond as you run the risk of contracting a waterborne bacterium, such as Weil's disease, which is carried by rats. The answer, if you have damaged skin and need to split or plant water lilies or pond-side plants, remove fish, or repair a damaged liner, is to wear protective tough, lined, PVC gauntlet gloves. They extend to the shoulder and have an elasticized hem.

HOUSEPLANT MITTENS

Keeping large-leaved philodendrons, Swiss cheese plants, and crotons glossy and free from dust can be time-consuming if you wipe them with a cloth coated with a leaf-shine chemical. Instead, do the job more quickly and easily by wearing a fleece mitt. Simply rub leaves lightly to remove dust and unclog pores.

LEATHER GLOVES

Durable and a good investment, most brands are constructed from four pieces: palm, fingers, front, and back. The best, however, have a seamless palm. Leather is excellent for rough work, such as pruning, sawing, and handling prickly shoots; the toughest are double- or triple-stitched. The palm should have two layers of thornproof cowhide, and seams must be on the outside to keep them from blistering your fingers.

When trying on leather gloves, flex your hands to check them for comfort. They must feel smooth. If there's a rough spot, look for a better pair. When leather gloves get wet, dry them slowly in a cool place. Never dry them them on a radiator, as they will stiffen and become uncomfortable to wear.

Cowhide gloves are a good choice as they have a tight and appealing grain. In tests to check their resistance to abrasion, cowhide was about a third more durable than deerskin or goatskin.

Pigskin is also called washable leather. It is tougher than cowhide and just as supple, but less attractive.

For hardworking hands

Waterproof gloves are useful for repotting and when working in damp conditions (left); thornproof gloves are helpful when pruning roses (center); durable all-purpose gloves (right) with a long cuff are ideal for heavy pruning, digging, and building work.

Goatskin and deerskin are a joy to wear but less durable than cow or pigskin, so keep these gloves away from roses and other prickly plants.

Sheepskin is a creamy white and softer to wear, but more easily damaged than other hides. Gloves made from it impart an elegant touch when you're using them to lightly tidy up borders. The lanolin they secrete keeps hands soft.

MODERN FABRICS

If you suffer from cold hands and your gloves take a long time to warm up, try hide gloves lined with the modern fabric Thinsulate. Its microfibers have a much larger surface area than most insulating materials so they trap air efficiently to keep fingers warm.

Both leather and hardwearing cotton canvas coated with heavy-duty crinkle latex will safeguard you from thorns and other sharp objects. They will also keep you dry. Choose a pair that snugly grips your wrists to keep out dirt.

If you're making a new garden, refurbishing a bed or border, and need to move rough objects, you'll want heavy-duty, abrasion-resistant gloves. Ideal are durable suede gauntlets with extended safety cuffs. The palm side of the middle two fingers should be a separate piece, reinforced with a welt at the seam.

Another glove that is strong, thornproof, and easy to work with has a heavy-duty cotton back, making it flexible, and a palm made out of Kevlar, a material found in flak jackets. An elasticized cuff will keep your hands clean.

If it's keeping dry in wet conditions that concerns you, but you also want a warm, comfortable and flexible glove that allows you to tackle all sorts of jobs, opt for cotton, jersey, or canvas.

Coated with a water-resistant substance, the lint-soft interior makes it a pleasure to wear. Most useful are those with a "gripping" palm.

HEAD AND FACE

You will need two hats: one to protect you from sunlight, the other to keep you dry. Guard against the harmful effects of UV-light with a wide-rimmed, ventilated white cotton or straw hat. If you prefer cotton, choose a non-crushable version that you can fold into a bag or pocket until you need it. Try a light, waxed, cotton hat, with or without a peak, for deflecting rain.

If it's cold and dry, keep your head warm with a deer stalker or conventional cap made from wool tweed or mixed fiber tweed. Warmer still is a fleece cap with ear muffs.

SAFEGUARDING YOUR EYES AND EARS

Power equipment can be extremely noisy, and, if cutting or shredding, can throw up splinters and debris that could damage your eyes. It is essential, therefore, to wear the correct protective garb.

Ear protection Ear plugs are effective against noise damage from most garden equipment, including mowers, but if you regularly use very loud power tools, seek out ear protectors that fit snugly over the ears and offer a greater degree of protection.

Eye protection Plastic goggles are relatively inexpensive and generally wrap around the side of the head to shield the whole eye area. Try them out, if possible, before you buy, to ensure that they fit properly, particularly if you wear glasses.

Proper headwear

It is sensible to don a hard hat (top) when pruning overhead branches or working at a height; goggles (center) will protect your eyes from flying foreign objects; keep your ears safe by wearing ear protectors (bottom) when using noisy power tools.

Safeguards & precautions

Certain garden tasks—such as mowing the lawn, trimming the hedge, and harvesting fruit from tall trees—have obvious risks. But even some of the most innocuous-sounding of chores, like hand weeding, are not without their hazards (insect bites, cuts and bruises, rashes, and allergies).

A FAMILY GARDEN

Children and pets can be curious and may not have a sense of danger, so it is sensible to take the following precautions: Lock away all chemicals, keep children well away from all lawn equipment both when you are using it and when it is in storage, make ponds safe by covering them with sturdy grids, and hang up tools, such as spades and forks, so they cannot be dislodged.

Ponds and pools are very appealing to children who love to look at their reflections in the surface of the water and try to spot fish. But you should always be extra-vigilant if the water is not fenced off or covered with a childproof grid. Such a grid, fixed to rigid beams firmly secured to the pond side, is almost invisible and can be easily installed. Plants grow well beneath and around it, and you can still enjoy the fish.

When the family is enjoying fine weather outside, don't forget to apply sufficient sunscreen and insect repellent, if necessary. Allergies are another common problem, particularly hay fever, so keep an eye on the pollen count.

Younger children love to dig in the garden. Ensure there are no poisonous plants within their grasp, and that they don't put soil-covered hands in their mouths. Also cover sandboxes when not in use so they are not soiled by neighborhood cats.

Install an adequate lock on your garden shed, so children can't wander inside unattended. It is also a good idea to keep your garden generally clutter-free to help prevent accidents.

Climbing the ladder

Never stretch out too far when standing on a ladder as this could cause you or the ladder to topple over. If you have a large area to tackle, keep moving the ladder so that you can easily reach the required spot.

Be careful with your barbecue grill: Position it away from sheds, fences, and overhanging branches, and keep younger children well away from the flames.

USING LADDERS SAFELY

Always position your ladder on a hard, flat surface—never on soft, bumpy, or sloping ground. If you are using a power tool or hedging shears on the ladder, don't overreach, as this could cause you to fall. Generally speaking, if you are standing on a platform higher than 6 feet with a hedge trimmer in your hand, you should have guard rails around you.

Make sure the ladder is tall enough for the job you want to do, as most accidents occur when ladders are too short. Keep your weight evenly distributed while climbing and working on the ladder. Avoid carrying equipment when you climb up, and when you reach

THE RULES OF TOOL SAFETY

Carelessly stored garden tools can cause some nasty accidents. The sharp points and cutting surfaces of forks, rakes, spades, bow saws and long-handled hoes are particularly dangerous—and children are most at risk. Accidents are less likely if you take the following precautions:

- Secure a tool rack of thick plastic-coated metal, with grippers for hand and long-handled tools, to the wall of a shed or garage.
- Hang forks, spades, and other long-handled tools so that their heads are almost touching the floor. Never store sharp-bladed or spiked tools upside down.
- Lock the shed or garage after safely storing your tools.

in flower or shrub borders, has large flat feet to keep it from sinking into the ground. It also has a nonslip platform with generous guard rails that allow you to lean forward from the platform and safely cut the top of the hedge.

WORKING WITH ELECTRICITY

Statistics reveal that the most common cause of garden electrical accidents is faulty electric lawn mowers, closely followed by hedge trimmers and lawn trimmers. The simplest way to protect yourself from danger is to use a ground fault circuit interrupter (GFCI). This will automatically monitor the circuit and stop the current from reaching you if you pick up a frayed or severed power cord, or if the machine's electrical insulation is damaged. Fit it to the tool or insert it between the plug and socket: When it senses a fault, it will cut off power, but it must be reset when

the top, with your weight balanced, ask someone to pass you the tool you need or take it from your belt.

One of the safest ways to cut a high hedge on uneven or sloping ground is to work from a steel platform with drop legs adjusted to make it level and stable. A stepladder version that can straddle or stand

Electrical safety

Always check power tools, including plugs and extension cords, before you use them outside, and make sure they are long enough to allow full mobility.

No hover bother

It's easy, when swinging a hover mower from side to side, to run over and accidentally sever the power cord. This won't happen if you fit snap-tight, rotating, bright yellow balls, a short distance apart, to the cord. When the machine touches a ball, with the electric cord inside it, it will roll harmlessly out of the way.

Breathe easy

Wear a mask when carrying out dusty work such as shredding. Some brands contain cartridges that filter out chemicals as well, which is useful when spraying.

a fault has caused it to trip. Other ways to reduce electrical risks are to:

■ Keep trailing cords as short as possible and well away from moving blades.
■ Get a qualified electrician to install outdoor waterproof sockets.
■ Make sure the extension cord is grounded.
■ Never use electric tools when it is raining.
■ Always disconnect a mower or trimmer from the power supply before examining the blades.

WORKING WITH CHEMICALS

Always read the labels on any product before you use it and follow the recommended instructions precisely. Even organic products can irritate the skin, breathing passages, or the eyes if splashing occurs. Never spray when it is windy. Remember to wear long pants, sleeves, and gloves when handling chemicals, and wash your hands and boots thoroughly when you're finished. Finally, many products are poisonous, so make sure you keep them well out of the reach of your children and pets.

PROTECT YOUR BACK

Whether you are reaching for inaccessible areas, hauling unwieldy equipment, or moving heavy containers, always take steps to protect your back. Always bend your knees when moving heavy objects, rather than trying to support all the weight from your back. And try to keep a straight spine when digging, too. If you're troubled by back problems, look into acquiring a back support.

CHAIN SAW WISDOM

A chain saw is a quick and efficient tool for removing small and large tree limbs, and sawing up logs. If you've never used one before, consult an expert before beginning.

You must also wear protective clothing that can "breathe" to keep you from getting hot and sweaty. Even if you intend to use a chain saw only occasionally, we recommend the following:

■ Helmet with mesh visor and ear protections
■ Jacket, ideally with protective blocking material—a matted fiber that clogs the mechanism and stops the machine should the blade of the saw get into the jacket
■ Chain saw mittens with blocking material in the back of the left hand
■ Seatless pants with all-around blocking material, to be worn over jeans or ordinary pants
■ Gaiters, with blocking material
■ Steel toe–capped boots

8

Gardening
with Ease

Specialized tools

Gardening can be very physically demanding, and the enjoyable exertions of a morning mowing grass, raking moss, and pulling weeds deserve the reward of a long, hot bath followed by a cool drink of iced tea. But if you find the mower unreasonably heavy after a few minutes' work or your back aches after a little light weeding then you should refine your tools to take the strain.

Help is at hand from tool manufacturers who have crafted a range of gadgets to help us tackle most jobs with ease, from mowing to hoeing, weeding to digging, and pruning to watering.

You can find implements to keep you from bending, kneeling, and overexerting your arms and hands, if you tire easily. Tools have been crafted for gardeners confined to a wheelchair or with a weak grip, and for those who are visually impaired. If standing upright for any period of time becomes difficult, choose a tool that lets you work from a sitting position, such as long-handled trowels and hand forks, specially-designed hoes and cultivators, weed knives with telescopic handles, and weeders.

If strength is an issue, remember that the more leverage you have with a tool, the easier it is to operate. Use ratchet pruners and loppers for pruning, and forks, trowels, hoes, and weeders fitted with pistol-grip handles. With such a multitude of operating methods, make sure you try all the tools within a section to find one that works best for you.

WEED CONTROL

Weeds are a perennial problem for gardeners, and unless you are exceptionally fortunate, you will have to deal with weeds germinating and competing with your cultivated plants for most of the year. If it's hard for you to find the time or energy to weed, you may

Lopping with ease

Cutting high branches or reaching deeper into a plant is made easy with the use of a ratchet lopper. Relax your upper body and arms to use loppers effectively.

decide to suppress weeds with a mulch of perforated plastic, pulverized bark, or grass cuttings. You should clear existing weeds before laying a mulch to avoid weeds flourishing underneath.

However, if you enjoy weeding—and many gardeners find it relaxing—you should consider several well-designed tools to keep intruders at bay.

HOEING WEEDS

Conventional push hoes and draw hoes require some effort, but not the golf-club hoe, which has three cutting edges for weeding, taking out seed drills, and earthing up potatoes. Its lightweight, aluminum alloy shaft has a comfortable contoured grip that you hold while you ease the blade back and forth through the

Practice your swing

Regular weeding with the golf-club hoe means never having to stoop. Small weeds will wither on the surface of the soil and may not need to be collected by hand.

soil to slice off weeds. The shape of the head allows you to work comfortably among border perennials and shrubs, and is less likely to damage plants than an orthodox hoe.

Push-pull weeders have serrated and double-sided blades that you can use with a push-pull action just below the soil surface. They are good for weeding in the vegetable plot or flower borders as they have side guards to protect nearby plants.

For rogue weeds growing on a patio or between paving, try a long-armed weeding knife, which you can use comfortably from a sitting position. It is essentially a strong steel blade with a hooked end, designed to pry weeds and moss from between paving slabs and other cracks.

EXTRACTING WEEDS

Harpoon-like weed extractors are great for removing those tenacious dandelions, along with other deep-rooted weeds. Push them into the ground close to the weed you want to dig up, and then twist and pull to extract the roots and all.

Weeding while standing

Long-handled flame wands prevent knee and back aches from weeding. Fueled by butane or butane and propane gas canisters, a flame wand is lightweight and easy to use.

KNEELING PRETTY

If you cannot bend or crouch, don't risk kneeling directly on the ground to weed. If you do, the pressure or strain may cause the fluid-filled sac in front of your kneecap to become inflamed. Guard against this by using a kneeling stool made from stove-enameled tubular steel or plastic. It has hand supports to help you get up or down, and a comfortable, soft, knee pad. If you turn it upside down—so that hand supports become legs—you have a seat from which to sow seeds, repot plants, or weed.

For greater mobility, strap on a pair of comfortable knee pads. Most are made from water-resistant, stretchy, high-density foam with adjustable fastenings to ensure a snug fit. No matter how wet the ground, you'll stay dry and eager to continue gardening.

DIGGING AND CULTIVATING

You can sprain your wrists from digging in the fall and hoeing in spring, especially if you are unused to these jobs. Both can also damage muscles in your neck, shoulders, or back. If you cannot garden as well as once you did, try using specially designed tools that take the strain and help you enjoy being outdoors!

Another way to extricate weeds without bending (but you'll need two hands) is to arm yourself with a plunger weeder. Simply position its cone of spike-like tines over a weed and push down on the foot plate. Twist gently and extract the weed quickly. Remove the trapped weed by pressing down on the plunger. You can fill the holes it leaves in a lawn by turning the soil plug and weed upside down and putting them back in the hole.

Similar in function is the weed-puller, made from rust-resistant steel with a cadmium-plated blade and claw, and a shaft with a trigger-like grip. Insert the blade beside the weed and loosen the plant by wiggling the tool around. Squeeze the trigger to make the claw grip the weed before levering it out. You can use it single-handed—but you'll need a strong wrist.

SCORCHING WEEDS

If hoeing or pulling up weeds seems like too much effort, why not burn them into oblivion with a flame gun? There are two types of burners: One is an electric gun that blasts air up to around 1200°F onto weeds, the other is a small burner connected to a propane gas cylinder. Whichever you use, tackle weeds in two or three bursts. Initially shrivel them, and then, a few days later, burn them off. Pernicious weeds sprout from below soil level and need treating several times.

Adapted handles

This bicycle-handled fork protects the wrists from strain while relieving soil compaction. Comfortable grips and a long handle mean you can stand upright while using it.

" What a man needs in gardening is a cast-iron back with a hinge in it."

CHARLES DUDLEY WARNER, WRITER (1829–1900)

SPADES AND FORKS

A new generation of longer, lighter spades and forks encourage a more upright digging stance, which may protect your back from discomfort or injury. Their curved shafts and inward-angled D-handles make digging and forking a safe pleasure.

There are two clever fork variations: One has four strong tines on the same plane and an easy-twist bicycle handle with comfortable grips. Use it standing bolt upright for removing weeds or breaking up compacted soil around plants.

The other variation, also used when standing, has four angled tines at the end of a long shaft that are twisted into the soil. This also comes with a bicycle handle. Use both throughout the year for loosening rain-compacted soil around border plants and shrubs, or for breaking up ground before raking to make a seedbed. You can also use it prior to planting bedding plants and perennials, or for incorporating granular fertilizer or organic mulch. Wipe blades clean with an oiled cloth.

CULTIVATORS

If you need to aerate and crumble your soil but have difficulty using a spade or fork, there are several tools that will help you do the job. A long-handled hand fork is great for teasing out weeds and aerating borders without bending too much. Its lightweight head and cranked, tubular shaft make light work of tilling a border.

Pistol-grip tools This family of tools is made up of forks, trowels, weeders, hoes, and cultivators. The heads are made of stainless steel to reduce soil adhesion, and a heavy-duty plastic handle is attached at right angles to the working head so you can grip the tool firmly in a stress-free position.

If you have weak hands or wrists, lock the tool into an arm-support cuff to harness forearm strength. Some manufacturers produce long-reach versions of the trowel, fork, cultivator, and hoe.

Soil crumbler A joy to use either standing up or sitting down, its four sharp, star-wheel tines at the front are connected to a rocking pendulum. In the process of pushing it back and forward you can pulverize lumpy soil 4 inches deep, and the blade at the back cuts the heads off weeds. It's heavy to lift—when not resting on the soil, but you can use it with one hand for tilling soil between vegetables or flowers, or for incorporating manure or fertilizer.

Automatic digging

This automatic digger allows gardeners to dig three times faster than their normal rate and with much reduced effort. A foot resting on the rear arm stabilizes the tool, while the arms do most of the work.

Tools on a budget

Tools are likely to be your biggest initial financial investment in gardening—but how do you decide which are important and which you can do without? Here we outline a basic tool kit for those on a budget.

If you're new to gardening, you are not alone in feeling bewildered by the array of tools available and daunted by the costs involved in buying a complete set.

One solution, especially if you are furnishing a house at the same time, would be to acquire a set of second-hand tools from family or friends or at garage sales.

If you are enthusiastic, however, you may prefer to buy new tools. If you've never gardened before and are not sure whether you will truly take to it, don't buy the best, for they may be abandoned later. If you find yourself wavering, choose sturdy, well-designed, and comfortable tools that are relatively cheap. Manufacturers grade their tools from high quality to utility, so there's a good range to choose from. Whatever basic set of cultivating tools you buy, look for carbon steel heads. Shafts or handles should be of lightweight polypropylene, steel, or wood.

Digging and cultivating
Your first tool should be a digging spade (see pages 12–17): Use it to turn over ground, make trenches, and create planting holes. It should be about 3 foot 4 inches long and have a D-shaped handle.

Your second most important acquisition will be a digging fork (see pages 18–19). Slightly shorter than a spade, but similarly constructed, it's invaluable for forking over and pulverizing heavy ground, crumbling soil for seed beds, shifting garden compost into a wheelbarrow, aerating a lawn, or loosening soil around plants. If you are digging a planting hole and come to a compacted stony layer, you will need a fork to pry out stones. Check that there are no sharp edges or protruding rivets that could blister your hands.

You will need a steel rake if you are preparing seed beds, sowing flowers or vegetables, or leveling a site for a lawn from seed or turf.

Building a tool kit
A set of tools passed down from a family member or friend can be a wonderful way to begin your own collection (left). Alternatively, buy new tools from a garden store (above), where you will be able to test the tools for size and comfort before making a purchase.

Buying new tools

Look for a tread—a flattened piece of metal—on top of the blade of a new spade (far left) to make digging more comfortable. A plastic watering can (center left) is perfectly adequate for new gardeners. Some tools, such as this "spork" (left), can do more than one job.

encounter stones or roots. For more on hand tools, see pages 33–37.

When buying a watering can, choose a sturdy plastic can, which will be far cheaper than metal and equally efficient. A 1½ gallon model, with capacity indicator lines and a detachable oval brass rose will serve you well. Unless your garden is very small, you will also need a hose. (See pages 42–48.)

Cutting and hauling

For pruning, deadheading and trimming, pruning shears are the best. Whether you choose a scissor-action bypass type or anvil model (pages 68–71), make sure that the hardened steel blades are coated with a non-stick substance to make cutting easier. Handles, if metal, should be plastic-coated.

If you have a lawn, you'll need a mower. This may seem like a big investment, but it will make your life infinitely easier. Choose a model that suits the size and layout of your garden. (See pages 58–63.)

It won't be necessary to buy a wheelbarrow unless you have a large quantity of soil to move, or are leveling ground or moving manure. If that's the case, choose a medium-sized, polypropylene barrow with a 10-gallon tray, pneumatic wheel, and one-piece frame with skids and comfort grips.

Check that there are 12 well-defined teeth and that the handle is the right length for you to use it smoothly and rhythmically. (See also pages 31–32.)

For tackling weeds from early spring to late fall you can rely on a Dutch hoe (see page 30). Also known as a push hoe, it's a tool that beheads weeds and aerates the soil around annuals, border plants, and shrubs.

Planting and watering

When it comes to planting, you will need a trowel. This small hand tool is ideal for working in window boxes, containers, and your beds and borders. Or consider a hand fork. Designed for planting bulbs, alpines, spring and summer bedding annuals, and herbaceous plants, it should have strong tines that won't flex or bend in heavy or compacted soil, or when you

The soil crumbler digs deeper in light, sandy soil than in heavy clay. Brush soil from the tines if they clog, and lubricate the spindle and pivot points with a spray of oil to keep them moving freely.

Mini cultivator These three-pronged devices are good for keeping small beds and borders tidy. Connect them to three lengths of handle (15 inches to nearly 5 feet) to aerate heavy or light soil between plants or loosen weeds so they shrivel and die. Some models have a weed-cutting blade attached to the tines.

PRUNING AND CUTTING

Pruning can be a tough job if you have weak arms and wrists, particularly when cutting through tough branches and stems. Conventional cutting tools including anvil or bypass pruners, loppers, and saws are efficient and relatively easy to use if you have average arm and wrist strength. But if you haven't, and still wish to prune trees, shrubs, climbers, and fruit trees, you should use ratchet cutters, long handles, or pulleys to give you greater leverage. Remember to grease pivot points with a lubricating oil to keep the action fluid.

RATCHET ACTION

Sturdy ratchet pruners greatly increase wrist leverage—30 percent less pressure is needed—and you are able to cut branches up to ¾ inch thick. You can prune thin shoots in one attempt while tackling thicker stems in stages. To operate, grip the stem with the pruners, squeeze the handles until you meet resistance, and then release pressure until you hear a click. This brings the stepped cutting device into play. Squeeze the handles again and the blade will bite further into the stem. One or two more bites (to a maximum of four) will sever the stem.

Ratchet pruners These are light and strong with handles made from heavy-duty plastic, or nylon and fiberglass. Anvil types have a hardened steel blade, which cuts onto a heavy-duty plastic anvil. In the case of the bypass pruners, a sharpened blade slices alongside an anvil.

Ratchet loppers These work on the same principle as ratchet pruners, in which robust, oval, tubular steel handles are bolted to a blade and anvil. Ratchet loppers allow you to cut 2-inch branches easily in several bites. Use them throughout the year to remove branches from shrubs and trees, or cut out thick shoots from the middle of rose bushes. You can replace both the blade and anvil.

CUT-AND-GRIP PRUNERS

These comfortable anvil pruning shears weigh as little as 7 ounces and are designed to slice through a stem and hold on to it: a big advantage when you're working from a sitting position. They have an easy, single-hand-operated catch that you can use for gathering flowers, or pruning roses and other shrubs.

Another model, which is long-shafted and versatile, has a trigger-grip handle and a 360 degree swivel cutting head. Use it for removing twiggy shoots from climbing roses, woody shrubs, holly, and other thorny bushes; and also for deadheading, cutting dead leaves from water lilies, and picking fruit.

COMPRESSED AIR PRUNERS

Operated by a compressor, the double-piston system, pneumatic pruner uses seven to ten bars of air pressure to make quick, clean—and most

Cutting back hard

Hard pruning this spring-flowering shrub is easy with a long-handled pruner. The longer the tool's arms, the greater the leverage it has to cut.

Step-by-step pruning

Ratchet pruners are designed for you to cut through tough shoots up to ¾ inch wide with ease. Squeeze the handles up to four times to cut through stems without twisting or straining your wrists.

importantly—effortless cuts. Use it from spring to fall for pruning fruit trees and bushes, ornamental shrubs, climbers, and roses.

Left hands If you're left-handed and find it awkward to use traditional pruners, you'll be pleased to know that one or two companies make a left-handed pruner. These bypass tools have an appetite for shoots as wide as ¾ inch, with a rust-resistant blade opened by an easily flicked catch.

Long-handled pruner If you've just moved and cannot reach the limbs of your new trees and shrubs to trim them, do the job using a long-handled pruner with a heavy-duty operating cord. The head is worked by two pulleys that double pruning power. Choose a head that you can lock into a lightweight telescopic pole, extending your reach to as much as 17 feet.

TRIMMING HEDGES

A boundary hedge is an asset: prized for the privacy it provides and the street noise it muffles. But it needs regular shearing to keep it looking good. If you have weak wrists or shoulders—or are not strong enough to use an electric hedge trimmer—use hedging shears.

There are several specially designed hedging shears with extra-long alloy handles to increase leverage,

Within reach

A 6-foot hedge in need of trimming won't be beyond you if you buy lightweight electric hedge trimmers with a telescopic arm.

Lawn tools for less effort

The lawn is one of the toughest parts of the garden to maintain. Ride-on mowers make light work of cutting the grass, as do cordless shears on ragged lawn edges.

which weigh as little as 2 pounds. Their carbon- or stainless-steel blades are razor-sharp and, despite repeated use, remain efficient for a long time before they need sharpening. Some blades are pressed with molded inserts to increase strength and reduce friction, and stainless-steel blades are replaceable. Use shears with telescopic handles if you need to reach across a wide hedge.

You may want to try gear-handled shears if your hedge is twiggy with thick shoots. These have a branch notch to help cut shoots up to ½ inch wide.

If you've moved to a yard with a high hedge and feel unsafe cutting it from a step ladder, there are extendable shears for this purpose. Essentially, a wavy-edged shear-head slots into a lightweight telescopic pole—head and pole weigh only 2 pounds and 12 ounces—and a strong cord operates the levered cutting head. Tug just once on the cord in order to cut a specific stem, and pull it repeatedly if you want to cut continuously. You will need both hands to hold the pole.

LAWN LORE

If you can't bend comfortably, suffer from arthritic joints, or experience back pain, you may find it difficult to mow, edge, rake, and aerate a lawn with conventional machines and tools. Some manufacturers are now aware of these problems and have designed mowers and other gadgets to meet your needs.

MOWERS

If you're in good health but have little energy, you will probably prefer a lightweight and maneuverable lawn mower. You can choose from a range of specially designed cylinder, rotary, or hover machines to suit

your budget, power supply, and taste in lawn stripes! Some 12-inch cylinder models weigh less than 22 pounds with four-blade cylinders and seven height-of-cut adjustments (from ½-1½ inches). Full-width rear rollers ensure those coveted green stripes, and energy-efficient motors keep the mowers moving.

There are several light rotary mowers with four wheels and a 12-inch blade. Most have large grass boxes, three cutting heights, and weigh 18 pounds.

Electric hover mowers are ideal for trimming banks and other uneven areas. They ride on a cushion of air and are usually "swept" across the lawn. A plastic or metal blade cuts the grass, which is left on the surface or sucked into a grass box. Smaller models weigh just 10 pounds with an 11-inch plastic blade, and have an adjustable height of cut. Some models are motorized and have a pivotal head to help you steer them.

TRIMMING LAWN EDGES

The handles of heavy, long-handled edging shears are often too short and, in bending awkwardly, the job becomes arduous and straining. The comfortable

"If only one were as good a gardener in practice as one is in theory, what a garden one would create."

VITA SACKVILLE-WEST, WRITER AND GARDENER (1892–1962)

answer is to use a single-shafted model rather than a conventional two-handled model. Swivel its blades into a vertical or horizontal position to cut edges or flat areas around paths, seats, and other objects.

Single-handed shears are for people who are not able to stand to manage a long-handled shear. With these you can kneel or sit—the easy, effortless, lightweight answer is a single-handed swivel shear. It cuts grass cleanly with spring-loaded, steel blades operated by a trigger-action lever. Rotate the blades—not your arm—through 180 degrees to neaten the sides of a lawn or flat areas that the mower can't reach. You can also use these shears for trimming topiary that is made from box, yew, or privet, as well as for removing soft shoots from alpines, heathers, and other shrubs.

Cordless shears are easier to use for cutting flat strips of lawn adjoining walls, fences, and garden sculpture. They are light with a robust motor, and have easily sharpened, hardened steel blades, which are specially coated in order to prevent them from rusting and accumulating dirt. You will, of course, have to kneel down to operate the shears. If you find that position awkward, try attaching a single-shaft guide-handle fitted with a safety switch.

Another satisfying and relatively effortless way to level grass around obstacles is to use a lightweight, electric nylon-line trimmer while standing upright. There is little or no pressure exerted on the back muscles and you can use it with one or both hands. Some models have a variable, easy-to-swing, wrist-supporting handle, designed to reduce fatigue while trimming at full reach.

You can rotate the handle of many models through 180 degrees for cutting lawn edges. If you are taller than average, fit a 6-inch telescopic handle extension to make trimming more comfortable.

RAKING MOSS FROM LAWNS
Removing moss and thatch from grass can be painful if you have a bad back, slipped disk, or muscular problem. Even raking may seriously aggravate the

Multifunctional wheelbarrow
If a single-wheeled wheelbarrow is difficult to balance, try a lightweight cart of UV-treated resin with two wheels and a stabilizer.

problem. But by using an electric scarifier you can keep a lawn aerated (free from clogging, dead grass) and in glowing, good health. This labor-saving ally has a jawful of hooked, steel teeth, a front roller with depth adjuster, and a grass box, which comes with a compactor to double capacity and cutting in half the trips to the compost bin. (You can even save the moss you collect to line hanging baskets.) With the scarifier's teeth set high, you can also pick up leaves to make leaf mold.

AERATING COMPACTED TURF
Periodically, especially in the fall, you should spike the lawn and compacted patches of heavy soil to let in air and revitalize root growth. If able, do this with a garden fork, stabbing the grass to the full depth of the fork's tines every 6 inches. Then use a steel rake to work into the holes a mix of sharp sand and topsoil.

An easier method for those with less energy is to use a hollow-tined aerator to create drainage holes up to $2\frac{1}{3}$ inches deep. Operate this by pressing your foot on to the aerator's platform to eject plugs of soil from tines at either end.

If using a hollow-tined device makes you breathless, strap a pair of spiked soles to your boots and walk slowly over the grass. The holes you make will help your lawn breathe more easily and allow water to percolate into it—and you may enjoy the exercise.

CARRYING WATER

The old-fashioned yoke our ancestors used showed how aware they were of the importance of distributing loads evenly when lifting and carrying. If you want to keep your back and spine in good shape, particularly while watering, it may not be wise to use a round, metal watering can. In holding it away from your legs to keep it from bruising them, it's easy to strain your back, arm, and wrist muscles. A rectangular plastic watering can, which holds around 9 pints is a far better choice for your back. You could also use two smaller cans, carrying one in each hand to balance the load.

WATERING WITHOUT A HOSE REEL

If bending causes you pain, forget about unwinding and winding up a hose reel. Instead, irrigate beds and borders with a porous pipe zig-zagged through them that has been buried 1 inch or so beneath the surface of the soil. When you want to water, all you have to do is connect a short length of hose from the outside faucet or water butt to the near end of the porous pipe that you have left protruding from the soil. Water feeds through the hose and onto the soil. Use it to water shrubs, flower beds and borders, window boxes, lawns, roses, vegetables, narrow flower beds alongside paths, hedges, and fruit trees.

This trick works best with water at low pressure, so open the faucet by only a quarter to half a turn to irrigate about 4 feet of soil on either side of the hose.

Watering wisely

Avoid round watering cans to protect your back, as holding full cans away from your body can cause strain. Opt instead for flat-sided plastic cans. Choose a handle that helps to tilt the can so that you do not twist your arm or shoulder as you water.

Computerized watering

Water can be transported from tap to flowerbed through an automated watering system. The hose, which can sometimes be buried under the surface of the soil, is pumped with water at preset times and quantities. This system is also helpful if you are often away from home.

Accessories to help you water the entire yard include straight, tee, and elbow connectors, in-line faucets, water filters, pressure reducers, and a double-check valve to prevent risk of water "back-siphoning" and contaminating your source.

HANGING BASKET WATERER

Choose hanging baskets that can be lowered when you need to water, or opt for one of the following easy options. Connect a hose to a lightweight spray wand. Choose a model that extends from around 2–4 feet. It should also have a finger tip on-off control and come with a spray head that delivers ultra-fine droplets for penetrating deep into the compost.

Alternatively, automate watering by installing a computer-regulated, drip-feed system. With this you can spray, mist, or drizzle plants, or accurately drip water into the soil to ensure it is moist at all times. The heart of the system is an electronic water timer that you can set to deliver a certain volume of water up to several times a day.

SETTING YOUR SIGHTS

If you enjoy the great outdoors, an inability to see clearly needn't spoil the pleasures that gardening brings you. With a little practice in orientation—aided by paths of varying textures, hand rails, focal points at a set distance apart, wind chimes, scented or bright shrubs—you will soon discover how easy it is to locate key areas.

Of course, there will be problems, but it's very satisfying when you resolve them. For example, cover the tops of canes and other thin plant supports with rubber or cork tops to make them safe.

FINDING TOOLS

A big problem in not being able to see clearly is that when you put down a tool, you are inclined to lose it. So, after using a trowel, hand hoe, pruner, or other

small tool—which should be vivid red or another bright color—don't put it on the ground, return it to a tool-belt holder.

Holders come in several shapes and sizes. Among them are three- and four-pocket tool pouches, three-pocket bib aprons, and two-pocket waist aprons. Most are made from durable, lightweight nylon with mesh pockets that allow soil to filter out. Edges and straps are often made of nylon webbing, and stress points are reinforced with rivets.

Buckets are excellent for holding hand tools and their usefulness is greatly increased if you strap a "carryall" around one. You'll be amazed at what you can transport around the garden without having to constantly walk to and from the house and shed.

A green hose can be invisible on a lawn—and it could trip you up. Why not use a bright yellow one instead? In winter, its color may even cheer you up!

Keeping in sight

If your eyesight is reduced, make sure your tools are highly visible. Return hand tools to your tool belt until you next need them (above). Green-colored tools and hoses that blend in with the lawn can become obstacles to trip over; instead seek out tools with bright colors that you won't miss (right).

9

Looking after
Your Tools

Safeguarding your tools

When you find a tool that works for you—whether it's a hoe, daisy grubber, or cuttings knife—hang onto it and protect it with a passion. If you lose or break it, you may never find another like it. Good gardening tools are your friends—they work with you to achieve reliable results with comfort and ease. Chosen carefully, after much deliberation, you want them to endure, and the longer you have them, the more you cherish them. They may require little more than a rub with an oiled cloth to protect them from rust, decay, and the eventual need to replace them. But it's knowing when to apply that oiled cloth that can save you substantial time, expense, and anxiety.

WASHING DIRTY TOOLS

Never put away used spades, forks, hoes, cultivators, and steel rakes without cleaning them first. This is particularly important if you garden on clay soil which coats tools with a hard, dry crust. Initially, wash them with the garden hose. If you can't hose them down—handles and all—use a bucket of water and a

The value of maintenance

Neglected metal tools need to be rubbed with oiled sand to remove patches of rust (above). When well oiled and cared for, your tools will last you a lifetime (right).

scrubbing brush. If they are only slightly soiled with mud, you can use a wooden or plastic scraper to remove it.

When metal blades and handles are clean and dry, wipe them with an oiled cloth or spray them with a petroleum-based lubricant and rust inhibitor. Alternatively, plunge spades and forks several times into a bucket of oiled sand before storing them. Preserve wooden handles by wiping them with a cloth soaked in linseed oil.

PROTECTING YOUR KNIFE

A clean, sharp knife is necessary for making cuts that will heal quickly when you propagate your plants by budding, grafting, layering, or taking cuttings. Wipe any sticky plant sap from the blade with a solvent based on mineral spirits, and follow this by rubbing the blades with an oiled cloth. Sap left on blades will usually turn black and make further cutting difficult. If the sap has been left to harden, remove it with an emery cloth or wire brush attached to a power drill.

When not in use, keep all cutting tools in a dry, cool place (out of the reach of children) where moisture won't attack and rust blades. After cleaning blades and other metal parts, coat them with a rust-inhibiting lubricant and squirt thin oil where blades pivot to keep them moving freely. Coat wooden handles with linseed oil.

MAINTAINING MOWERS

Whichever lawn mower you have, its efficiency will be determined by the maintenance you give it. A cursory wipe of the blades will not be good enough after

SPRING CLEANING YOUR MOWER

Carry out all cleaning jobs on a firm, paved, or concrete surface. Use a stiff brush to remove caked-on grass and soil from blades, the grass-collection box, and rollers. If you have a rotary or hover mower, remove mud from under the canopy. The best tool for this is a wide plastic or wooden scraper. Follow by rubbing all metal areas with a rag soaked in thin oil and lubricate the chain and other moving parts. Rest the machine on a thick layer of newspapers to catch mud, grass clippings, and drops of oil. Store in a dry, airy shed or garage.

---

cutting the lawn. If you want your machine to serve you well, you must spend more than a few minutes cleaning and checking it.

Electric machines Do not attempt to clean an electric mower until you have unplugged the machine and disconnected the power supply. Then remove mud and grass clippings with a stiff brush and oil the machine's moving parts. Check the cords for cuts. If you find one or more, repair them with a waterproof connector or, ideally, replace the cord.

When the cutting season ends, examine leads for loose connections and tighten if necessary. If cords are worn or inner plastic-coated wires are visible—no matter how slightly—repair them with waterproof connectors or replace them altogether.

Gas mowers Before cleaning your gas-powered machine in the manufacturer's recommended way, use up the fuel in the carburetor to prevent it from going stale by leaving the engine running with the drive disengaged and the fuel tap shut off. The engine will cut out once it has used the fuel in the carburetor.

Check the oil level, too. If the oil is black, it is time to change it. If you find yourself frequently filling up the sump, check now for leaks, as oil dripping onto

For extra security

When not in use, keep your knives and other cutting implements in a holster. This will not only help to keep the blades sharp, but will also protect you from accidental cuts.

your grass will kill it. Periodically examine the air filter with a view to cleaning it if it's dirty or changing it if it's become damaged.

When the cutting season ends, put your gas-powered mower to bed properly. Drain off all fuel to avoid leaving any in the cylinder and replace the engine oil with a fresh supply. Clean the spark plug with a wire brush and set the gap to comply with that recommended in the manufacturer's handbook.

Battery-powered mowers After cleaning the machine, immediately recharge the battery. Every two weeks, check the level of distilled water in the battery cells and, if necessary, fill it up. Use a rag to clean dirt from battery terminals. If dry, rub them with petroleum jelly.

When the cutting season ends, remove and clean the battery and fill up the cells with fresh, distilled water. Recharge the battery and store it in a warm, dry place, ideally on a wooden base, to keep it above the floor.

Rotary and hover mowers The blade of a rotary or hover mower may be a long strip of metal with two cutting edges, or a triangular blade that you remove from a rotating, circular, metal disc. Either should be sharpened by securely clamping them into a vice and taking a flat file to them.

Take care, when sharpening strip blades, to remove the same amount of metal from each end. It's necessary that the blade remains level when you have sharpened it. Test the blade for balance by suspending it on a nail or screwdriver: If one end points up, sharpen the other until the metal bar is horizontal.

A stitch in time...

Spray lubricating oil onto metal joints to prevent them from becoming stiff (left). Always remove any grass cuttings trapped under the blade of the mower so they don't clog the machine (center). Use a rag soaked in linseed oil (right) to keep wooden handles smooth and prevent cracking.

Cylinder mowers Unlike rotary and hover mowers which cut by slashing grass, a cylinder blade rotates against a fixed bottom blade and cuts with a scissor action. Refine the cylinder by attaching a sharpening strip to the bottom blade and adjusting the cylinder so that it lightly brushes against it. If you are not sure about how to do it, you can have the cylinder sharpened professionally.

Curing rust Remove any rust by rubbing it with emery paper or a wire brush. Restore treated areas by painting them with red oxide and follow this with an undercoat and gloss topcoat.

SHARPENING YOUR TOOLS

All cutting tools must be sharp. If not, they are hard to use and leave ragged cuts on your plants that may become diseased. Blunt knives can also be dangerous, for they tend to slip away from a shoot rather than cut into it properly.

The sharper your pruning shears and loppers, the cleaner the cuts and the quicker they will heal. If pruning saws aren't sharp, they will bind up.

> **"He that would perfect his work must first sharpen his tools."**
> CONFUCIUS, PHILOSOPHER (551–479 B.C.)

You should always keep spade and hoe blades sharp. Blunt tools take longer and require more effort to slice through the soil.

Sharpening equipment To sharpen your knives, pruning shears, loppers, scythes, sickles, axes, and shears, you will need a medium-fine flat file—some brands are embedded with diamond particles. Alternatively, to produce a razor-sharp edge, invest in a grinding stone. Choose from coarse or fine grades of synthetic or natural grinding stones. Whichever you use, moisten it with water, oil, or gas before use; its instructions will tell you which lubricant to use when you buy it. Otherwise you won't build up a paste of stone particles, necessary for honing a blade, and the stone will quickly wear out.

Hand sharpening If practical, dismantle your pruning shears, loppers, and hand- and long-handled shears to sharpen them more easily, setting the blade in a vice. You can sharpen a blade more accurately this way than by holding it in your hand. Remember, if you are using a file, hold the tip in one hand and the handle in the other, and lightly press it against the blade. Push it away from you. Remove it from the blade when you've finished a stroke and then begin again. A file is not designed to be used backward.

If hand sharpening takes too long or is physically demanding, tighten the blade in a vice and create a sharp new edge in seconds by using a grinding stone connected to an electric drill. Sparks will fly, so wear safety goggles and gloves.

After sharpening all blades, coat them with water-repelling oil—especially if the air is damp—to keep rust from attacking them and reducing their efficiency.

Chain saws These require precise sharpening with a round file, or they won't cut well. If your hands are unsteady or you find it difficult to file at the correct angle, use a precision filing tool mounted securely on a work bench.

Hedge trimmers Brush the blades of electric hedge trimmers with mineral spirits to remove clogging prunings and sticky sap before wiping them clean and spraying them with an antirust lubricant. Examine the cord for abrasions and repair it with a waterproof connector, or replace altogether.

STORING YOUR TOOLS

Never store garden tools in a random heap. It's not easy to find the one you want and searching for it is exasperating and dangerous. In discovering hand shears and other small hand tools tucked away behind larger ones, a carelessly-positioned spade, fork, rake, hoe, or saw may fall upon you. Helpful guidelines when storing tools include:

- Don't hang your tools too high. It's physically and also hazardous! You could be hurt by a garden fork that slips from your fingers.
- Tools, no matter what shape or weight, should remain where you put them.
- Position them so that handles or working heads are just above floor level.

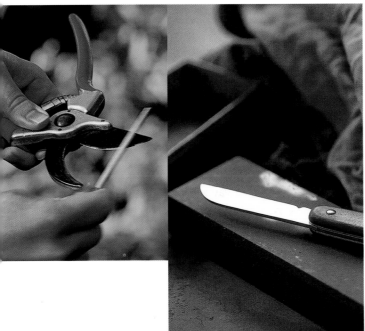

Guidelines for sharpening

Be careful, when you are using either a file (far left) or a sharpening stone (left), to draw it across the blade, from tip to heel, at the same angle at which the blade was sharpened when it left the factory.

Handy hooks

Secure a tool rack on one wall of your shed so that you can suspend light implements off the floor and out of harms way (left). Bulky equipment should be hung from large, securely fixed hooks (above).

Storing methods The easiest way of storing tools is to screw strong and generous hooks onto a wide wooden backboard secured to the wall of your shed or garage. Alternatively, use dowels, angled slightly upward and securely glued into place. Yet another way is to fix a 'peg board to the wall and hang tools from hooks locked into it. Nails and screws must be long enough and their heads large enough to ensure that tools cannot be dislodged if you brush against them. Check regularly that the nails have not loosened.

If you use snap-in steel grippers—some kinds glide on a track for random spacing—do not overload them with tools heavier than they are designed to support. Large, heavy-duty hooks are useful on their own for storing bulky tools, or linked, for ladders and wheelbarrows.

Tool bags Hung on a shed, garage, or greenhouse wall, a simple pocketed strip of burlap, about 3 x 1 feet in size, with a handle, makes a perfect home for small tools. Here you can store your hand forks, trowels, cultivators, pruning shears, knives, sheep shears, and widgers, which, when you've finished with them, are easily misplaced. If your tool kit consists of a selection of interchangeable working heads that slot into a common short, intermediate, long, or telescopic handle, then storing heads and handles is easy with a specially-made support rack. Screwed vertically to a wall, it comes with sturdy, upward-facing sockets for tool heads. There are handle holders, too.

SHEDS

A shed should be cool and airy in summer, warm and dry in winter, with light flooding through generous windows. Home to a variety of implements, it should also be well-organized. You must know where a particular tool is and be able to find it easily.

Size and siting The larger a shed, within reason, the easier it is to store tools—many of which you haven't yet bought! So think of a size, then double it.

In addition to garden tools, you may want a work bench, power equipment, and space for bicycles. Shelves will help maximize your floor space. A shed must be in proportion to your beds and borders. It

"The man who has planted a garden feels that he has done something for the good of the whole world."

CHARLES DUDLEY WARNER, WRITER (1829–1900)

must not overshadow your neighbor's garden. It should be as close as practical to the house, because if you hide it away at the end of a garden, you will be less inclined to use it in bad weather.

If your garden just isn't large enough for a shed, protect a wide range of tools from weather and theft in a storage chest of selected pine, waterproofed with an acrylic-based primer. The lid should be mineral-felted and come with profiled sills to keep out rain.

TYPES OF SHED

There are three basic structures: apex-roofed, pent-roofed, and dual-purpose. The big advantage of an apex shed is that its pitched roof, with a central ridge, allows you to build a generous loft for storing long, bulky, or rarely used items.

A pent-roofed shed, which is normally set close to a wall or fence has a flat top that gently slopes backward. Though it lacks the visual appeal of a pitched-roof structure, it is less expensive.

The dual-purpose shed, a hybrid combining the assets of a pent-roofed design and a greenhouse, is a good compromise if you haven't enough room for both structures, but enjoy propagating plants.

DO YOU TAKE YOUR TOOLS FOR GRANTED?

- Have you "mislaid" a garden tool in the last year?
- When was the last time you cleaned your lawn mower or changed its oil?
- Do you regularly give cleaned knives, pruning shears, and loppers a rub with an oiled rag to protect them from getting rusty?
- When not being used, are your tools stored out of harm's way?

If the answer to any of these is yes, then ten minutes at the end of each gardening session can save you money, time, and effort that would be better spent on gardening!

Wooden sheds Softwood and the more expensive western red cedar are traditional, very popular, and retain heat well. If you opt for softwood, ensure that it is pressure-treated with preservatives to inhibit decay. After assembling the shed, coat it annually with preservatives. Western red cedar is rot-resistant and doesn't need preserving. But, its glowing reddish-brown wood will turn a silvery hue if you don't paint it once a year with a cedar stain.

Concrete A robust, concrete shed is best positioned close to the house, rather than in the middle or back of the garden—where its hard lines are incompatible with beds, borders, and lawns. Soften walls, usually of exposed aggregate or imitation brick, by coating them with a weather-resistant paint and climbing plants.

Metal It's not the first material you might think of when buying a shed, but models constructed from hot-dipped, galvanized steel, finished with baked-on paint are remarkably handsome. They are robust, with large sliding doors, and have a long and useful life. There are apex and ridge models to choose from.

Though walls are usually windowless, most models have translucent roof panels to ensure that plenty of light illuminates your tools and work bench.

Glossary

Aerate Digging or forking compacted soil to help air percolate down to warm it and to improve root growth.

Anemometer A three-cupped instrument that pivots on a vertical spindle to record the speed of the wind.

Aneroid A portable barometer that can measure atmospheric pressure without the use of any fluid.

Apex roof Found in sheds and other buildings, this is a pitched roof with a central ridge that works to give you extra attic storage space.

Barometer An instrument that measures atmospheric pressure and records changes in weather or altitude.

Besom A broom that is made by tying a bundle of birch or heather twigs to the end of a pole with wire. Use it for sweeping up bulky areas of trash.

Biodegradable Material that decomposes into simple elements when attacked by bacteria and other biological processes.

Capillary matting Highly water-absorbent synthetic fiber on which pots are firmly placed. Moisture is drawn from this fiber up into the compost.

Cloche A temporary glass or plastic structure that is placed over outdoor plants to hasten and protect their growth, or to warm the soil before sowing or planting.

Clute-cut glove A glove designed so that the palm is made from one seamless piece of material. This ensures that the wearer's hands have a roomy, comfortable fit.

Compost activator A nitrogen-based substance like manure, fertilizer, or comfrey leaves but with additional enzymes and fungi, which are used to accelerate the decomposition of organic waste into fertile, crumbly, and nutrient-rich humus.

Deadhead Cut or pinch off the faded blooms of bedding plants, roses, and border perennials to ensure that they channel all of their energy into producing more shoots and flowers, rather than unwanted seeds.

Dibber A short, cone-shaped tool, which often has a metal end, handy for making holes in the soil or compost, for inserting cuttings, or for planting seedlings, young leeks, and brassicas.

Double digging A method of turning over the soil in which a wide trench is taken out and the soil is then dug to a depth of two spits (each a spade blade deep).

Enzymes A group of complex proteins that are produced by living cells and that trigger biochemical reactions. Some compost activators contain enzymes.

Fulcrum The pivot of a lever, such as the wheel spindle of a barrow.

Galvanized Steel or iron coated with a layer of rust-proof zinc.

Gore-tex Durably waterproof but still breathable fabric. Each square inch has an amazing nine billion holes, which keep rain out but also allow the water vapor from perspiration to escape.

Ground fault circuit interrupter An adapter that protects you from being electrified. It works by detecting an earth fault, and then cutting off the power in under 40 milliseconds. Fit it between your power tool and the mains socket.

Hormone-rooting powder/liquid A synthetic plant hormone—such as naphthyl acetic acid or indole butyric acid—that stimulates root development. Dip your cuttings into it before inserting them into rooting compost.

Hygrometer An instrument used to measure humidity levels.

Lacewing chamber A wooden box that is designed to attract and provide winter protection for beneficial insects called lacewings, which feed on greenflies and many other sucking pests.

Leaf mold Crumbly, blackish brown material formed by decomposing a heap of leaves. Add it to seed and potting compost or use it as a soil-conditioning mulch.

Microbe A beneficial or harmful bacterium that can only be seen with a microscope.

Microclimate A small area in which the atmospheric conditions affecting organisms differ from the general climate of the surroundings.

Needle bearings Small roller shaped anti-friction bearings found in the wheel of a barrow that help it to run smoothly.

Neoprene A form of synthetic rubber that is resistant to oil and aging, and is often used to waterproof clothing.

Nonreturn valve Fitted between the hose and the water source, this valve prevents back-siphoning. It's a good idea to invest in one if you are using a liquid fertilizer, as it prevents contamination of the water supply.

Oasis Also called floral foam, oasis is a cellular plastic material. The green version, when it is used wet, can soak up almost 30 times its volume of water. The brown or gray form tends to be used dry, for dried or artificial flower arrangements.

Oscillating hoe For removing weeds and loosening compacted soil, this has a push-pull, square-shaped rocking head.

Pent roof This is a term that is usually applied to a shed whose roof slopes gently backward.

Permanent wilting point This is the point when a lack of moisture in the soil forces a plant to use up so much fluid from its own cells that it dies.

Pheromone trap Usually used to control the codling moth, this is a sticky device that is impregnated with the scent of a female moth and then hung in fruit trees to lure and kill male moths.

Pneumatic Containing compressed air. A pneumatic wheelbarrow tire, for example, which ensures a smooth ride.

Polartec A breathable fleece fabric often used for base and middle layers of outdoor clothing. Sweat is wicked away from the garment to leave skin feeling dry.

Polypropylenes A family of tough, flexible synthetic thermoplastic materials, which are made by polymerizing propylene.

Pricking out Transferring crowded seedlings from a pot or a tray to where they will have more room to grow.

Pruning shears Anvil type: A straight-edged cutting blade that closes onto a flat bar of metal—often brass—known as the anvil. Bypass type: Two curved blades brush past one another, cutting with a scissor action.

Saddle joint This joint is one way of fixing a spade head to its handle. Two straps come up from the head, lie flat against the front and back of the handle, and are secured with rivets.

Scarification A method of improving growth by using a flexible rake to remove any dead grass and moss from a lawn.

Scion A shoot cut taken from one plant (variety) with the intention of grafting it onto another plant (stock).

Setting out Planting a tree, shrub, border perennial, or any other plant where you want it to grow.

Silica A refractory, insoluble material notably used in the manufacture of glass, ceramics, and also abrasives.

Single digging A method of turning over the soil in which only the fertile top layer of soil is dug, and to a depth of only one spit or spade blade.

Socket joint This is a joint that is frequently used to join a spade's head and handle. The handle fits into a circular hole at the top of the head and is well secured there with rivets that are driven through the shaft.

Spit The depth of a spade blade, usually about 10–12 inches. Soil is usually dug either one or two spits deep.

Sprinkler A watering device that fits on to the end of a hose and sprays droplets over a wide area.

Stamped metal A spade blade that is fashioned from a metal sheet.

Subsoil A zone of usually infertile, poorly textured, and poorly structured soil around 12 inches below the surface.

Tanalize A process of preserving wood in order to keep it rot-free for many years.

Tang-and-ferrule A method of attaching the shaft or handle of a tool to the head, commonly used to make hand tools. The tang is a sharp point on top of the head that fits into the base of the shaft. The ferrule is a metal ring that fits over the joint to hold it closed and to stop the wood from splitting.

Tetanus Also known as lockjaw, this illness is caused by a bacterium found in manure and other organic material. Given the opportunity, it can easily infect injuries, especially those with a deep, dirty, and airless puncture wound.

Thinsulate An insulating fabric whose microfibers have a much larger surface area than most alternative materials. It is often used to line gloves.

Tilth A 2–3-inch layer of fine, crumbly soil that is produced by raking, and in which seeds are sown.

Tine The prong of a fork, rake, or other soil-cultivating implement.

Topsoil The upper 9–12 inches of dark, fertile humus-rich soil in which plants tend to grow.

Trug A lightweight garden basket that is usually made from sweet chestnut, willow, birch, or plaited rush.

Velcro A fastening consisting of two strips of nylon: one having tiny hooked threads; the other a coarse surface into which the threads can mesh.

Weil's disease Another name for leptospirosis, a bacterium that can cause kidney failure, jaundice, and meningitis, and is transmitted to humans by rats and other animals. Ponds may also harbor it.

Acknowledgments

Picture researcher Sandra Schneider
Indexer Michele Clarke
IT support Paul Stradling
Production Nigel Reed, Karol Davies

Val Bradley would like to thank the many companies who were so helpful in supplying information, and Steve, Chris, and Nick for their patience.

Carroll & Brown would like to thank Pamela and Michael Stewart-Murray, Cornwall, UK, for allowing us to photograph in their garden, Paul from Earthworks, and Abdul and Hanis Bharmal at Carpenders Park Nursery.

Picture Credits

t = top; c = center; b = below; r = right; l = left; GPL = Garden Picture Library

Suppliers

Recommended suppliers for gardening equipment:

ACE Hardware
2200 Kensington Ct.
Oak Brook, IL 60523-2100
630-990-6600
www.acehardware.com

Armstrong Garden Centers
2200 E. Alosta Ave. Suite 200
Glendora, CA 91740-4673
626-914-1091
www.armstronggarden.com

Black & Decker
1-800-544-6986
www.blackanddecker.com

Earthmade Products
P.O. Box 609
Jasper, IN 47547-0609
1-800-843-1819
www.earthmade.com

Home Base Home Improvement
Warehouse
3345 Michelson Drive
Irvine, CA 92612
1-800-481-BASE
www.homebase.com

Home Depot
2455 Paces Ferry Road
Atlanta, GA 30339
770-433-8211
www.homedepot.com

House2Home
3345 Michelson Drive
Irvine, CA 92612
1-877-980-7467
www.house2home.com

IKEA
Plymouth Meeting Mall
498 W. Germantown Pike
Plymouth Meeting, PA 19462
610-834-1520
www.ikea.com

Lehman's
P.O. Box 41
Kidron, OH 44636
1-888-438-5346
www.lehmans.com

Lowe's Home Improvement
Warehouse
P.O. Box 1111
North Wilkesboro, NC 28656
1-800-44-LOWES
www.lowes.com

McGuckin Hardware
2525 Arapahoe Avenue
Boulder, CO 80302-6795
1-800-558-6753
www.mcguckin.com

The Natural Gardening Company
P.O. Box 750776
Petaluma, CA 94975-0776
707-766-9303
www.naturalgardening.com

Orchard Supply Hardware
6450 Via Del Oro
San Jose, CA 95119
408-281-3500
www.osh.com

Restoration Hardware
15 Koch Road, Suite J
Corte Madera, CA 94925-1240
1-877-747-4671
www.restorationhardware.com

Roger's Gardens
2301 San Joaquin Hills Rd
Corona del Mar, California 92625
1-800-647-2356
www.rogersgardens.com

Sears
3333 Beverly Road
Hoffman Estates, IL 60179
1-800-549-4505
www.sears.com

Smith & Hawken
Hangar No. 4, Hamilton Landing
Novato, CA 94949
1-800-940-1170
www.smith-hawken.com

Stihl
536 Viking Drive
Virginia Beach, VA 23452
1-800-467-8445
www.stihlusa.com

Target
1-888-304-4000
www.target.com

Total Tools & Garden Supply
Box 5019 PMB 117
305 N. Second Ave.
Upland, CA 91786
1-877-572-3277
www.toolsandgarden.com

True-Value Hardware
8600 Bryn Mawr
Chicago, IL 60631
1-877-474-9054
www.truevalue.com

Index

acid soil 93
activators, compost 114
aerating lawn 141–2
aerating soil 10, 32, 135, 138
aerators
   compost 115
   lawn 65–6, 142
algae clearance from ponds 103
alkaline soil 93
allergies 127
American shaker brush 97
American shovel 17
ankle boots 119–20
anvil pruner 138
anvil pruning shears 14, 69–70
apex shed 151
aprons 121, 143
aquaplanters 103
arches 92
armillary sphere sundial 50
arms, protection 120–1
artificial fertilizers 112
artificial flowers 89
asparagus knife 35
atmospheric pressure measurement
   51
automatic vent openers for greenhouse 53
automatic watering systems 143
axes 79
   sharpening 149

backpack sprayers 15
bags
   fruit harvesting 45
   self-opening and collapsing 109
   transport 108–10
bamboo stakes 91, 92
barbecue safety 127
basket frames for rose training 15
baskets
   for harvesting 45, 104, 110
   for ponds 103
battery-powered cordless hedge
   trimmers 74
battery-powered mowers 59
   maintenance 148
bedding mattock 19
beet fork 18
besom broom 96–7
bicycle-handled fork 134, 135
billhooks 79
bird protection of fruit 44–5
blade adjuster on mowers 61
blade and half-anvil pruning shears
   70
blades
   billhooks 79
   cleaning 147
   hedge trimmers 149
   knives 73
   mowers, maintenance 147, 148
   pruning shears 69, 71
   saws 75

scythes 78
   sharpening 62, 148–9
   shears 74, 140
blinds for greenhouse 52–3
blowers 99–101
bobby pins for topiary 77
bonsai tools 28–9
boot rack 120
boots 119–21
   steel-toed, for chain saws 78
border fork 18, 21
border shears 64, 65
border spade 12
bouquets 89
bow saws 75
brambles, scything 79
branches
   pruning 75
   shredding 101
brass fittings for hoses 43
bristles on brooms 96, 97
brooms 96–8
   besom 96–7
   children's 123
   handles 96, 97–8
   patio 97
   push 96, 97–8
brush hooks 79
brushes 96–8
   American shaker 97
   bonsai 29
   for mower maintenance 147
bubble polythene 53
buckets 92, 143
   cut flowers 88
   fruit harvesting 45
   transport 108–10
Budding, Edwin Beard 60
budding knife 15, 45, 73
   for flower arranging 89
budgeting for tools 136–7
bulb planters 85
bulbs
   dibber for 86
   planting 84
butts 48
Buxus sempervirens 76
bypass pruners 138
bypass pruning shears 68–70

calibrated trowel 84
canes 92, 143
canvas baskets 110
canvas tray in wheelbarrow 107
carbon-steel tools 23
   hand forks 85
   trowels 85
carts 107–8
celery, earthing up 35
cement bags, moving around 107
chain saws 78
   safety 129
   sharpening 149
chemicals, safety 127, 129

chest, protection 120–1
chicken wire
   compost bins 113
   flower arranging 88, 89
   topiary 77
children
   in gardens, safety 127
   tools 122–3
      digging 122
      plantings 123
      rakes 123
chisel for bonsai 29
choosing tools 20–1, 23
   hand tools 27, 33, 36
   pruning shears 69–71
circuit interrupters 128
clamps for bonsai 29
cleaning tools 146–8
clearing water in ponds 103
cloche tunnel 35
cloches 91
clogs 119–20
clothing, protective 118–26
   chest, arms, and legs 120–1
   children's 123
   feet 119–20
   hands 124–5
   head and face 126
   for using chain saws 129
cold frames 91
colored tools for easy finding 143
comfrey leaves for composting 114
compacted turf, aerating 141–2
compost bags, moving around 107
compost bins 113–15
   insulation 114–15
   making 114
   siting 115
compost fork 115
compost tumbler 113–14
composting 112–15
   compost bins 113–15
   making a heap 115
   materials for 114
   success with 114–15
   turning materials 115
compressed air pruners 138–9
computerized watering system 143
concrete mixing, shovel 17
concrete shed 151
conifer pruning 74
connectors for hoses 43, 143
conservatories 52–3
container plants
   drip-feed system for 47, 143
   water needs 40, 41
containers 92–3
   bonsai 29
convector heaters 53
cordless shears 140, 141
cords, checking 147
cork toppers for canes 143
Cornish spade 17
costs of tools 23, 136

covers for ponds 103
cowhide gloves 125
craft knife for flowers 88
cultivating, specialized tools for
   134–5, 138
cultivators 32, 35
   mini- 138
   pistol-grip 135
   specialized 135–6
   three-prong 37
   wheeled hoe 27, 30
cut-and-grip pruners 138
cutters for bonsai 29
cutting tools 68–71
   axes and hatchets 79
   billhooks 79
   chain saws 78
   for flowers 88
   hedge tools 73–5
   knives 71–3
   large 75, 78–9
   loppers 71
   pruning shears 68–71
   saws 75, 78
   scythe 78–9
   shears 73–4
   shredders 79
   sickle 79
   small 71, 73
   specialized tools 138–40
   see also pruning *and under specific*
      tools
cuttings
   from shredders 101
   knives for 73
   propagators 90–1
cylinder mower 56, 58, 60, 61
   maintenance 148
   specialized 140

daisy grubber 65
deadheading roses 14
deerskin gloves 125
dew on lawn 57
D-handles 21
dibbers 35, 85–6
digging
   double 10, 16
   need for 10
   safety 129
   single 10, 13, 15
digging tools
   children's 122
   specialized 134–5, 138
digging up plants 13
digital thermometers 51
diluters for hoses 14, 44
disabilities, tools for 142–3
dispenser, seed 34, 35
distilled water for mower batteries
   148
dividing plants 85
dollies for transporting 107
dot matrix shading film 53